# THE MISSING BAPTISM

## RICHARD E SNOWDON

# THE MISSING BAPTISM

RICHARD E SNOWDON

# Ambassador International
GREENVILLE, SOUTH CAROLINA & BELFAST, NORTHERN IRELAND

www.ambassador-international.com

# The Missing Baptism



ISBN:     978-1-62020-229-6
eISBN:    978-1-62020-372-9


Printed by Bethel Solutions


**Ambassador International**
Emerald House
427 Wade Hampton Blvd
Greenville, SC 29609, USA
www.ambassador-international.com

**Ambassador Books and Media**
The Mount
2 Woodstock Link
Belfast, BT6 8DD, Northern Ireland, UK
www.ambassadormedia.co.uk

The author can be contacted at the following e-mail address:
 themissingbaptism@btinternet.com

# **CONTENTS**

# PREFACE

This book has been written primarily for those who are already Christians. If the reader is unsure of where he or she stands with God, or professes no faith at all, the Appendix at the rear should be read carefully before attempting the rest of the book. It contains a brief explanation of mankind's true history, the origin of sin and its presence in every person upon earth. The Gospel (or *good news*) of God's grace in the Lord Jesus Christ is shown to be the *only* way of salvation from sin's penalty and power.

How few who profess to be Christian seem to feel a genuine grief over the spiritually impoverished condition of even the true Church in Britain. Of a minority who understand from Scripture and the signs of the times that we are living in the last of the last days, even fewer have a burden for genuine revival. Perhaps wearied and even intimidated by wave after wave of spiritual deceptions, many of the Lord's people have retreated into what Dr. Martyn Lloyd-Jones once described as "dead orthodoxy" (the condition in which an assembly's doctrine is largely correct, but where there is an absence of vital spiritual life of the sort evident in the Book of Acts and during periods of true revival). Revival is even considered impossible by some, due to the darkness of the days and the imminence of the Lord's coming for His Church. Others recoil at the very mention of 'revival' because of its recent association with numerous false prophecies, often from the lips of those who deceptively teach that a triumphant Church will establish the Kingdom of God on earth prior to the return of the Lord Jesus Christ.

Further to this, many of the Lord's people have either grown up in, or have long attended, assemblies and churches that teach that the Gifts of the Holy Spirit were withdrawn once the Scriptures were completed. This teaching is generally known as 'cessationism'. 'Isms' are rarely wholly scriptural and this one is no exception. The aim of this book is to help the reader see that 'cessationism' does not stand up to a scriptural analysis. This author firmly believes that, though there are a number of reasons for the feeble condition of the Church in the West, the dogma of 'cessationism' looms very large among them. In such thinking, the possibility of a fresh outpouring of the Holy Spirit is discounted and therefore not prayed for, thus leaving believers trying to serve the Lord in their own strength. The results (or rather lack of them) are painfully clear to see.

"The Missing Baptism" is written with a heartfelt desire to encourage God's people to search the Scriptures afresh and seek the Lord concerning the vital matter of being filled or baptised with the Holy Spirit. It is a precious promise of God to *all* believers, which makes it all the more grievous to observe its widespread denial in Western 'Bible believing' churches. This is not a new teaching – C. H. Spurgeon once said that there is nothing new in theology except that which is false! Rather, it is a Biblical truth in great need of being recovered and taught accurately and authoritatively from our pulpits.

The current, popular teaching that all believers are

automatically baptised with the Holy Spirit at the point of conversion is challenged in the light of Scripture. The principle of 'sola scriptura' (i.e. that Scripture alone is our authority for all doctrine and practice within the church) will undergird the arguments in this book. Church history, testimonies, analogies and illustrations may be used, but will always be subordinate to the 'sola scriptura' principle. Objections from cessationists will also be examined according to the same principle.

At such a critical time in world history, are *you* content with the powerless version of 'Bible-believing Christianity' that has come to be regarded as normal in Britain?  Do *you* accept 'second hand' teaching as truth and know little or nothing of the presence and power of the living God in your midst?  If not, *"who knoweth whether thou art come to the kingdom for such a time as this?" (Esther 4:14)*

The urgent need of the hour is for men who will contend for "the whole counsel of God", rather than *most* of it. We have many otherwise good Bible teachers and preachers who expound *most* of God's counsel to us, but far too few who will fearlessly proclaim *all* of it! Such men will have been prepared by God over many years and will be no strangers to affliction, trial and unpopularity.  Knowing a measure of freedom from 'the fear of man', they will both live and proclaim *all* that the Lord has taught them irrespective of traditionalised interpretations of Scripture. The apostle Paul did not shrink back from his responsibility: *"For I have not shunned to declare unto you **all** the counsel of God." (Acts 20:27)*

May God in His mercy raise up more men in the same Spirit as Paul.

CHAPTER 1

# DIAGNOSING THE NEED

In his 1959 series of sermons on revival, Dr. Martyn Lloyd-Jones commenced with a message entitled, "Diagnosing the Need". No doubt drawing on his training as a medical doctor, he realised the folly of embarking upon a course of treatment for a spiritual malady without first making an accurate diagnosis as to the nature of that condition.

Whilst much could be said about the enfeebled state of the modern Church in Britain and the West in general, it is surely due in large degree to the accelerating apostasy so clearly prophesied in the Bible for the last days of this present age. Much has been said and written by faithful men, exposing the unbiblical roots of the latest church growth movements as well as the false teachings of the men behind them. Therefore there is no intention to reiterate these at length in this book.

The scope will largely be confined to that part of the professing church that we call the True Church, Remnant or Body of Christ. From here on in, I'll refer to this Remnant as the Church and the broader bounds of Christendom as the professing church. The professing church, of course, includes both genuine believers and unsaved church members.

Before going any further, we need to establish whether there is anything wrong with the Church in Britain. How can we do this? When doctors examine a patient, they keep in mind a set of baseline parameters such as blood pressure, pulse, temperature and breathing that are considered normal. If the patient's vital signs differ significantly, the doctor will conclude that something is wrong!

Having established that something is abnormal, the doctor must now take any other symptoms into account and diagnose the cause of the disorder. How can we use this analogy to help us examine the condition of the Church? What we need is a baseline or reference point to show us what the Church should be like. Clearly, this is to be found in the Scriptures.

The book of Acts has been called "The Young Church in Action". This was the title that J.B. Phillips gave to his new translation of the book in 1955. It might also justly be called "The Acts of the Holy Spirit", since it was only through His enabling that any of the early Church's miraculous feats were possible. This book gives us a tantalising glimpse of what the Church should be like. In the following excerpts from J.B. Phillips' Translator's Preface, we begin to see a comparison being drawn between those early believers and their modern counterparts in the West.

*"It is impossible to spend several months in close study of the remarkable short book, conventionally known as the Acts of the Apostles, without being profoundly stirred and, to be honest, disturbed."*

*"Yet we cannot help feeling disturbed as well as moved, for this surely is the Church as it was meant to be."*

"*No one can read this book without being convinced that there is Someone here at work besides mere human beings.*"

"*In the pages of this unpretentious second book, written by the author of the third Gospel, the fresh air of Heaven is plainly blowing, and to turn from the vitality of these pages to almost any current Christian writing, be it a theological book or a Church periodical, is to bring tears to Christian eyes.*"

"*When we compare the strength and vigour of the Spirit-filled early church with the confused and sometimes feeble performance of the Church today, we might perhaps conclude that when man's rigidity attempts to canalise the free and flexible flow of the Spirit he is left to his own devices.*"

"*Of course it is easy to "write off" this little history of the Church's first beginnings as simply an account of an enthusiastic but ill-regulated and unorganised adolescence, to be followed by a well-disciplined maturity in which embarrassing irregularities no longer appear. But that is surely too easy an explanation altogether. We in the modern Church have unquestionably **lost** something. Whether it is due to the atrophy of the quality which the New Testament calls "faith", whether it is due to a stifling churchiness, whether it is due to our sinful complacency over the scandal of a divided Church, or whatever the cause may be, very little of the modern Church could bear comparison with the spiritual drive, the genuine fellowship, and the carefree[1] unconquerable courage of the Young Church.*"

---

1       Original 1955 text used the word 'gay' here, which didn't then have the modern connotation.

Clearly, this translator realised that the modern professing church does not compare favourably with the young Church in Acts. Notice in the last excerpt that he concludes that, *"We....have unquestionably **lost** (emphasis added) something"*. At this point in the diagnosis, he is not sure of the exact cause of this loss, but makes some suggestions. However, in the previous excerpt, I believe he correctly identifies a major difference between the early Church and that of today. They were Spirit-filled and, with few exceptions, we are not.

But why have so few Western Christians been baptised with the Holy Spirit? I believe the late David E Gardner gives us the answer in his book, "The Trumpet Sounds for Britain", Volume 3 – "The Alarming Apostasy and Its Inevitable Consequences". After dealing with that part of the professing church which, due to its liberal or modernist theology, preaches only a social "gospel", he goes on to deal with so-called "Bible believing" Churches.

*"It is the teaching of Scripture that needs to be recovered in the free Churches throughout the land as well. For there, also, we regrettably find much false teaching. Some of them are found to be totally dead and lifeless because they deny the need of the power of the Holy Spirit today. Some even go so far as to say that miracles, signs and wonders, and all the New Testament gifts of the Holy Spirit, were withdrawn at the end of the apostolic age. They have no authority whatsoever for saying this. The preaching in the New Testament days was always accompanied by mighty acts of power. God Himself bore witness to the preaching by mighty signs and wonders, by many miracles which he wrought, and by gifts of the Holy Spirit sent down from heaven. The faithful preaching of the Gospel is always meant to be accompanied by such mighty acts of power today."*

David E Gardner clearly believed that the culprit was false teaching. God willing, we shall go on in subsequent chapters to demonstrate from Scripture that he was right. However, a note of warning might be needed here. Some reading Gardner's description of churches that are, *"totally dead and lifeless"*, might not recognise their own meeting to be in that category. Citing their many programmes, loud music and exuberant worship, they would not readily identify themselves as *"totally dead and lifeless"*. Still others, whilst not exhibiting noisy activity, but often considering themselves to be the pinnacle of doctrinal correctness, fail to see the staid nature of their gatherings. Perhaps not surprisingly, many believers who have grown up in such meetings come to regard their experience as "normal" Christianity.

As always, the only reliable touchstone with which to measure our assemblies is not by our own opinions or by comparing them with other fellowships, but by holding them up to the light of Scripture. In our day, programmes, loud music and exuberant worship are all too often produced by the energy of the flesh and have little or nothing to do with the Holy Spirit. On the other hand, meetings that are mostly doctrinally sound but stolid in character rarely exhibit the "living water" of the Holy Spirit's activity in their midst. These would come into the category Dr Martyn Lloyd Jones termed "dead orthodoxy". In all cases, there is an urgent need to test how God views the situation, rather than relying on our own preferences and opinions.

The church of Laodicea had a high opinion of itself, thinking it had no need of anything, but our Lord told them,

*"Because thou sayest, I am rich, and increased with goods,*

*and have need of nothing; and knowest not that thou art wretched, and miserable, and poor, and blind, and naked: I counsel thee to buy of me gold tried in the fire, that thou mayest be rich; and white raiment, that thou mayest be clothed, and that the shame of thy nakedness do not appear; and anoint thine eyes with eyesalve, that thou mayest see.  As many as I love, I rebuke and chasten: be zealous therefore, and repent."* (Rev 3:17-19)

The Laodicean church's main problem was its spiritual blindness. It saw no cause for self-examination and repentance, but our Lord saw all too clearly. Most prophetic scholars are agreed that the predominant characteristic of the professing church in these last of the last days is Laodicean. Ironically, it is possible to be Laodicean in a noisy, emotionally hyped-up meeting, or in a highly orthodox but staid meeting, or indeed, in anything between.

It is always interesting to read what men who have been greatly used of God have said about these matters. Former China Inland Mission director, the late J Oswald Sanders, once preached a message to some new missionary candidates in which he said *"The problem with the Church is that it is stuck between Calvary and Pentecost, theologically and experientially. We understand and have experienced Calvary, but do we understand the meaning of Pentecost either theologically or experientially?"*

Hudson Taylor, the founder of the China Inland Mission said the following at a New York conference, *"God's power is available power. We are a supernatural people, born again by a supernatural birth, kept by a supernatural power, sustained by a supernatural food, taught by a supernatural Teacher from a supernatural Book."*

He then went on to say, *"We have given too much attention to methods and machinery and to resources and too little to the source of power, the filling of the Holy Ghost. This, I think you will agree with me, is the greatest weakness of the Church today. We have been commanded to be filled with the Spirit."*

Dr Martyn Lloyd Jones once famously said to his congregation, *"I want to talk to you today about the baptism of the Holy Spirit. You may call it what you want, but I want to know, have you experienced the fullness of the Spirit? I know all of you listening to me come as I do from a Reformed background. But it's not good enough. I know that all of you would want to say to my question about the Holy Spirit, 'Well, we got it all at conversion; there's no need for any more experience.' Well,"* said Martyn Lloyd-Jones, *"I have only one other question to ask you. If you got it all at conversion, where in God's name is it?"*

This last example from Dr Martyn Lloyd Jones well illustrates the problem in the Western Church. Multitudes of believers are taught, and consequently believe, that "they got it all at conversion". The question that the Doctor put to his congregation is a fair one. If they did, as they assert, "get it all at conversion", it is reasonable to expect to see evidence of this.

What would this evidence be? We have only to read the accounts in the book of Acts to see the effects of the Baptism with the Holy Spirit on first the Apostles and then the early believers. It achieved precisely what the Lord Jesus Christ said it would.

*But ye shall receive power, after that the Holy Ghost is come upon you: and ye shall be witnesses unto me both in Jerusalem, and in all Judaea, and in Samaria, and unto the uttermost part of the earth. (Acts 1:8)*

The Apostles were indeed clothed with power on the day of Pentecost, which resulted in bold and dynamic witness for the Lord Jesus Christ. It is vital to note that this was boldness and dynamism that they did not possess before the Holy Spirit empowered them. Lest any should object that this was only for the Apostles, Peter says the following as part of his sermon to the crowds:

*Then Peter said unto them, Repent, and be baptized every one of you in the name of Jesus Christ for the remission of sins, and ye shall receive the gift of the Holy Ghost. For **the promise** is unto you, and to your children, and to all that are afar off, even as many as the Lord our God shall call.* (Acts 2:38-39)

Notice how Peter links the receiving of the Holy Spirit (in the same way that they had just experienced) with a promise. What promise was this?

*Therefore being by the right hand of God exalted, and having **received of the Father the promise of the Holy Ghost**, he hath shed forth this, which ye now see and hear.* (Acts 2:33)

The Lord Jesus Christ also gives us the answer:

*And, behold, I send **the promise of my Father** upon you: but tarry ye in the city of Jerusalem, until ye be endued with power from on high.* (Luke 24:49)

*And, being assembled together with them, commanded them that they should not depart from Jerusalem, but wait for **the promise of the Father**, which, saith he, ye have heard of me.* (Acts 1:4)

Our Lord clearly identifies the "Promise of the Father" as being the enduing "With power from on high" and goes on to explain in the next verse that this will happen when, *"….ye shall be baptized with the Holy Ghost not many days hence." (Acts 1: 5)*

In every case we read of in the book of Acts, whether Apostles or early converts, the enduing "With power from on high" produced remarkable and eminently noticeable results. Dear reader, can you with scrupulous honesty assert that this is what we observe in our day whenever a person is converted to Christ? Yet modern "sound doctrine" continues to declare that "you get it all at conversion"! One senses that there is also a very common tendency to reduce the Scriptures to the low level of our own experience rather than humbly seeking God to lift us up to the level that He has taken such care to describe in His Word. Clearly, this is to give our own experience a higher authority than the Word of God.

It can be very interesting and instructive to read the first impressions of the Western Church gained by a believer from a part of the world where persecution is the norm. When Chinese Christian, Brother Yun, finally escaped from China to the West, he expected to find a strong and vibrant church which in former generations had taken the Gospel to China with incredible faith and tenacity. What he actually found deeply saddened him. This is what he said in the book, "The Heavenly Man", Chapter 25, "Reflecting on Four Years in the West".

*"On some occasions I've struggled while speaking in Western churches. There seems to be **something missing** that leaves me feeling terrible inside. Many meetings are cold and lack the fire*

*and presence of God that we have in China."* He goes on to say: *"I pray that God might use the Chinese church to help the Western church rise up and walk in the power of the Holy Spirit."*

Not many years ago a British visiting speaker came to speak at the Brethren assembly that I then attended. He came to tell us about his involvement with the work of the Egyptian assemblies in the midst of very real opposition and danger. What we heard was both thrilling and challenging. In drawing an unfavourable comparison between the Egyptian believers and those in the UK he ventured to point out one of the reasons for this. Concluding one remark on teaching in the UK he said, *"…… why, we're afraid to even mention the Holy Spirit!"* Quite so! Whilst it might surprise some readers, this comment was actually quite daring in such circles.

Another interesting observation is that whenever and wherever there has been a genuine move of God by His Spirit, there has always been an upsurge of opposition. It's not that we relish having a brick thrown through the window at our meetings, or something worse. However, the lack of serious opposition to our meetings and work must surely be another indicator that, in reality, there is very little to oppose!

What then, is our diagnosis? It surely doesn't take extraordinary powers of observation to reach the same conclusion as J.B. Phillips when he said, *"Very little of the modern Church could bear comparison with the spiritual drive, the genuine fellowship, and the carefree unconquerable courage of the Young Church"*.

In the next chapters we'll turn our attention to uncovering some of the reasons why we are in the state that we are.

# CHAPTER 2

# A CHURCH THAT DOES NOT KNOW ITS OWN BIRTHDAY

In the art of navigation, it is of crucial importance to know *precisely where* one has set out from. Get this wrong and, no matter how skilled the subsequent navigation, there will be an *error* built in from the start. It seems to me that it is just here that so many of us have gone wrong.

You might ask if we can or should apply a navigational analogy concerning point of origin to the Church. After all, does it really matter exactly when the Church was born? I hope to show that it matters a great deal.

Have you ever noticed how often God reminded Israel of her history in the Old Testament?

*The feast of unleavened bread shalt thou keep. Seven days thou shalt eat unleavened bread, as I commanded thee, in the time of the month Abib: **for in the month Abib thou camest out from Egypt**. (Exodus 34:18)*

The above verse is one of many in which God reminds Israel of her history. Notice the historical precision with which their Exodus is tied to the month Abib. God is concerned with historical accuracy in His Word because, very often, weighty matters hinge upon a chronological order of events or even specific dates. These reminders are particularly prominent in the Prophets during times of spiritual declension. When God's people have an incorrect understanding of their origins, doctrinal error and wrong practice become inevitable.

Before moving on, it would be a pity not to dwell briefly on the subject of "leaven" in the above verse. A whole study could be devoted to this fascinating topic. Suffice to say that in Scripture "leaven" is always representative of evil, either in doctrine, practice or both. Just before their Exodus from Egypt, the Jews were given instructions concerning the Passover and Feast of Unleavened Bread. They were to make a thorough search of their houses and get rid of any leaven. For the next seven days they were only to eat unleavened bread. Does this not have something to say to us? As Christians, we should feed upon *the true bread from heaven* (John 6:32), which is the Word of God. We are soon to undergo an exodus, not out of Egypt but out of this world at the Rapture. Over the years the teaching of God's Word has become 'leavened' in many respects through various erroneous teachings. It is remarkable how even true believers can hold irreconcilable views on many matters. Opposing views cannot both be true. In some cases the truth may lie elsewhere, rendering *both* opposing views false. As we near our Lord's return, I believe He would have us search out our beliefs for any areas of 'leaven' and sweep them away. Leaven may have been taken on board from books or by listening uncritically to our favourite pastor, preacher or teacher. There is a regrettable tendency even among true Christians to put men on pedestals, treating their words as infallible. By doing so, we create our own 'pope' who must not be challenged. Leaven can only be identified by a prayerful use of the Word of God, read without wearing the distorting spectacles of denominational prejudice or traditionalised interpretation.

*We have also a more sure word of prophecy; whereunto ye do well that ye take heed, as unto **a light that shineth in a dark place**, until the day dawn, and the day star arise in your hearts:* (2 Peter 1:19)

Just as the Jews would have used a lamp to search the dark corners of their homes for leaven, so we must use the Scriptures to illuminate the murky recesses of our wrong understanding in certain areas. The rewards for obediently making the effort will be neither small nor few! The Scriptures encourage us to be like the "Bereans", who *were more noble than those in Thessalonica, in that they received the word with all readiness of mind, and **searched the scriptures daily, whether those things were so**". (Acts 17:11)

This "Berean" principle of searching the Scriptures to check whether what we read or hear from Bible teachers and preachers is true or not (i.e. searching for leaven) has never been more important than in our day. There is an all-out assault on the Bible as the Word of God and its place as our sole authority on all matters of doctrine and practice in the Church. We are surely well into the Biblically predicted End-Time apostasy of the professing church. Whilst there is nothing new in this with regard to the errors of Roman Catholicism and much of the Protestant church, we are now witnessing a wholesale departure from biblical truth by many churches that call themselves "evangelical". The very name "evangelical" once had a very distinct meaning (that is, governed by the authority of Scripture alone), but current trends have rendered it virtually meaningless.

But now we must return to look at the particular leaven that is responsible for God's people failing to receive His promised power for service.

How many times have you heard preachers and Bible teachers use expressions such as, *"Now, when the Church was born on the day of Pentecost……"* or *"When the Holy Spirit came to form the Church at Pentecost……"* etc.? I've lost count of the number of times I've heard this sort of thing said. The extraordinary thing is that nobody seems to question it! We treat it as a "given" in our understanding, perhaps because it has been repeated so many times. Is this what the Bible really teaches though?

Let us now look at this notion that the Church was born on the day of Pentecost as asserted by so many and test it from Scripture like a noble "Berean". A close examination of Acts Chapter 2 will reveal that nowhere does it say that the Church was born on the day of Pentecost.

*Then they that gladly received his word were baptized: and the same day **there were added unto them** about three thousand souls.* (Acts 2:41)

What we read here is that 3000 people were **added to them**. What was the nature of this group to whom all these extra people were added? It was a body of men and women that included the Apostles, Mary the mother of Jesus, His brothers and many other believers, totalling about 120 (Acts 1:14-15). It was the infant Church **already in existence.**

This should immediately raise some questions. Someone will quote Romans 8:9 and point out that nobody can be a Christian unless he or she has the Holy Spirit. They would be quite correct in saying that.

*But ye are not in the flesh, but in the Spirit, if so be that the Spirit of God dwell in you.* **Now if any man have not the Spirit of Christ, he is none of his.**  *(Romans 8:9)*

They would then go on to say that since the Holy Spirit was not given until Pentecost, the assembled group of 120 could not have been Christians in the true sense until that day. To answer this objection we need to dig a little deeper into the Scriptures. In fact we need to be those who *"rightly divide"* the Word of God.

*Study to shew thyself approved unto God, a workman that needeth not to be ashamed,* **rightly dividing the word of truth.** *(2 Timothy 2:15)*

Many cessationists are very good at rightly dividing the Scriptures when dealing with weighty matters such as the doctrine of salvation or of the Second Coming of our Lord Jesus Christ, but seem curiously reluctant to exercise a similar rigour when dealing with the full doctrine of the Holy Spirit.

How then are we to show that the 120 were indeed already Christians and therefore constituted the infant Church? In answering this question we shall also see the true day on which the Church was born. From Pentecost we need to retrace our steps by fifty days to examine events on the day of our Lord's resurrection from the dead.

*(John 20:19) Then the same day at evening, being the first day of the week, when the doors were shut where the disciples were assembled for fear of the Jews, came Jesus and stood in the midst, and saith unto them, Peace be unto you.*
*(John 20:20) And when he had so said, he shewed unto them*

*his hands and his side. Then were the disciples glad, when they saw the Lord.*

*(John 20:21) Then said Jesus to them again, Peace be unto you: as my Father hath sent me, even so send I you.*

*(John 20:22) And when he had said this, **he breathed on them, and saith unto them, Receive ye the Holy Ghost:***

*(John 20:23) Whose soever sins ye remit, they are remitted unto them; and whose soever sins ye retain, they are retained.*

From John 20:22 we can see that the disciples received the Holy Spirit in the evening of the day of resurrection. Our Lord Jesus' words here are not a prophecy of the coming of the Holy Spirit fifty days later at Pentecost, but rather an indication of what was taking place there and then as signified by His breathing on them. A wonderful parallel with the creation of man has been observed here.

*And the LORD God formed man of the dust of the ground, **and breathed into his nostrils the breath of life**; and man became a living soul.  (Genesis 2:7)*

Notice that it was only after God breathed into the man that he had life. In the same way God's new creation, the Church, only came into being as a living organism after Jesus as God the Son breathed the Holy Spirit into the assembled group of disciples. This was the moment that the Church was born and not the day of Pentecost.

No true believer would deny that the Lord Jesus Christ is the Head of His body, the Church. In other words He is one with His body and His body is one with Him. To help us understand this we have only to look at the connection between our own head and body. They are joined together in a vital union with the head controlling the rest of the body. This brings us to an interesting thought; when a baby is born, normally the head appears first followed by the rest of the body. It seems almost superfluous to say that the body appears on the same day as the head and not fifty days later. When God said that He would greatly multiply a woman's sorrow in conception and bringing forth of children, thankfully He didn't have a fifty day labour in mind! Why am I saying all of this?

After His resurrection our Lord Jesus Christ is described as the "firstfruits":

*But now is Christ risen from the dead,* **and become the firstfruits** *of them that slept.*  (1 Corinthians 15:20)

*But every man in his own order:* **Christ the firstfruits**; *afterward they that are Christ's at his coming.*
*(1 Corinthians 15:23)*

When Christ was raised from the dead He became Head of His body, the Church. It is surely only fitting that His body be born on the same day. If His body was not to be brought into being until the day of Pentecost, the Lord Jesus Christ would be a Head without a body for 50 days. Knowing something of God's marvellous wisdom and precision in all His acts, it seems totally incongruous that He would have allowed such a state of affairs. Nevertheless, the main proof that this was not the case lies in the fact that our Lord Jesus Christ breathed the Holy Spirit into His disciples on the evening of that first day of the resurrection.

Before we leave this matter I believe it is necessary to

answer one more possible objection. Based on the verses below some have objected that the Holy Spirit could not have been given on the day of the resurrection because Jesus had not yet been glorified.

*Nevertheless I tell you the truth; It is expedient for you that I go away: for if I go not away, the Comforter will not come unto you; but if I depart, I will send him unto you.  (John 16:7)*

*(But this spake he of the Spirit, which they that believe on him should receive: for the Holy Ghost was not yet given; because that Jesus was not yet glorified.)  (John 7:39)*

The clearest indication that the disciples did indeed receive the Holy Spirit on the resurrection day is in Jesus' own words:

*And when he had said this, he breathed on them, and saith unto them, Receive ye the Holy Ghost:  (John 20:22)*

In order for all these verses to be true, something must have happened during that day, after our Lord was raised from the dead and before He appeared to the disciples in the evening. Does the Bible give us any indication of what this might have been? For the answer we need to visit the empty tomb early on resurrection morning with Mary.

*(John 20:15) Jesus saith unto her, Woman, why weepest thou? whom seekest thou? She, supposing him to be the gardener, saith unto him, Sir, if thou have borne him hence, tell me where thou hast laid him, and I will take him away.*
*(John 20:16) Jesus saith unto her, Mary. She turned herself, and saith unto him, Rabboni; which is to say, Master.*
*(John 20:17) Jesus saith unto her, Touch me not; **for I am not yet ascended to my Father**: but go to my brethren, and say*

*unto them,* **I ascend unto my Father, and your Father; and to my God, and your God.**

*(John 20:18) Mary Magdalene came and told the disciples that she had seen the Lord,* **and that he had spoken these things unto her.**

We need to notice here the real reason that our Lord Jesus told Mary not to touch Him. He said that it was because He had not yet ascended to His Father. She was told to go and tell the rest of the disciples that He was ascending to His Father. This was in the present tense and was not a prophecy of his final Ascension to Heaven, which was to be 40 days later. So why did he have to ascend to His Father just after His resurrection? The following words of Jesus to his disciples in the evening of the resurrection day provide the key to the answer.

*And he said unto them, These are the words which I spake unto you, while I was yet with you, that* **all things must be fulfilled,** *which were written* **in the law of Moses,** *and in the prophets, and in the psalms, concerning me.* *(Luke 24:44)*

Bible students understand that the Old Testament contains many "types" and "shadows" of our Lord Jesus Christ in His various roles and offices. Whilst these Scriptures contain the "types", Jesus Christ is the "anti-type". What "type" was Jesus fulfilling when he ascended to the Father on that resurrection day? It was the Feast of Firstfruits.

*(Leviticus 23:9) And the LORD spake unto Moses, saying,*

*(Leviticus 23:10) Speak unto the children of Israel, and say unto them, When ye be come into the land which I give unto you, and shall reap the harvest thereof, then ye shall bring* **a sheaf of the firstfruits** *of your harvest unto the priest:*

*(Leviticus 23:11) And he shall* **wave the sheaf before the**

**LORD**, *to be accepted for you: on the morrow after the sabbath the priest shall wave it.*

*(Leviticus 23:12) And ye shall offer that day when ye wave the sheaf an he lamb without blemish of the first year for a burnt offering unto the LORD.*

This sheaf of the firstfruits was to be "waved" before the LORD to give God thanksgiving and glory for the early or initial harvest, which anticipated the much greater harvest to come. What a wonderful picture of our Lord Jesus Christ in His resurrection as the firstfruits from the dead, giving promise of a tremendous harvest of souls to come!

So if the Church already existed, what was the purpose of Pentecost? The Lord Jesus Christ gives us the answer:

*And, behold, I send the promise of my Father upon you: but tarry ye in the city of Jerusalem,* **until ye be endued with power from on high.** *(Luke 24:49)*

Notice that He doesn't say, "*....tarry ye in the city of Jerusalem, until ye be* **formed into My Church from on high.**"

At the beginning of this chapter we asked whether it really mattered precisely when the Church was born. I hope that it has now become clear that it matters a great deal! To say that the Church was born at Pentecost is to misunderstand entirely God's purpose on that day. It is a leaven that has thoroughly permeated the thinking of probably the majority of believers in the West.

# CHAPTER 3

# GOD'S PURPOSE IN PENTECOST

First of all it is important to understand that Pentecost is primarily one of the seven feasts or 'appointed times' that God instituted for His people Israel. There is nothing arbitrary concerning the date in the Hebrew calendar when God poured forth His Holy Spirit in partial fulfilment of Joel's prophecy. It is another instance of the marvellous chronological precision of God's dealings with His special nation.

However, it is not the purpose of this book to dwell on that remarkable aspect of His Word. More gifted men than I have written books and recorded audio teaching on Israel, her feasts and related topics. Our aim is to examine God's purpose in Pentecost as it relates to those early Christians and to all believers since then.

Throughout most of the Lord Jesus' earthly ministry, the disciples displayed spiritual dullness and slowness of understanding even though they knew the Old Testament Scriptures. No doubt we would have been duller still had we been there in the flesh! However, after Jesus rose from the dead this began to change very much for the better. The two disciples on the road to Emmaus are a good example of how the Lord plugged all those gaps in their comprehension.

*(Luke 24:25) Then he said unto them, O fools, and slow of heart to believe all that the prophets have spoken:*

*(Luke 24:26) Ought not Christ to have suffered these things, and to enter into his glory?*

*(Luke 24:27) And beginning at Moses and all the prophets, he expounded unto them in all the scriptures the things concerning himself.*

Later that same evening, when Jesus appeared to the rest of the disciples, He marvellously dealt with their ignorance.

*(Luke 24:44)  And he said unto them, These are the words which I spake unto you, while I was yet with you, that all things must be fulfilled, which were written in the law of Moses, and in the prophets, and in the psalms, concerning me.*

*(Luke 24:45)* ***Then opened he their understanding, that they might understand the scriptures,***

At this point they finally had a clear understanding of who Jesus was and what was the purpose of His first advent. We might suppose that they were now ready to take the Gospel into the world, but no! Just a few short verses later, Jesus gave the disciples a vital command.

*And, behold, I send* ***the promise of my Father*** *upon you:* ***but tarry ye in the city of Jerusalem, until ye be endued with power from on high.*** *(Luke 24:49)*

The following verses from Acts chapter 1 further illustrate this command.

*(Acts 1:4)  And, being assembled together with them,* ***commanded them*** *that they should not depart from Jerusalem,*

***but wait for the promise of the Father,*** *which, saith he, ye have heard of me.*

*(Acts 1:5)  For John truly baptized with water;* **but ye shall be baptized with the Holy Ghost** *not many days hence.*

*(Acts 1:6)  When they therefore were come together, they asked of him, saying, Lord, wilt thou at this time restore again the kingdom to Israel?*

*(Acts 1:7)  And he said unto them, It is not for you to know the times or the seasons, which the Father hath put in his own power.*

*(Acts 1:8)*  **But ye shall receive power, after that the Holy Ghost is come upon you:** *and ye shall be witnesses unto me both in Jerusalem, and in all Judaea, and in Samaria, and unto the uttermost part of the earth.*

Let us note that this was indeed a command and not a suggestion or an option. One can only conjecture what would have become of the Church if they had disobeyed that instruction. If they had reasoned the same way that many in today's Church do, they might have said, "But we already have the Holy Spirit, what more do we need?" They would have remembered that forty days earlier Jesus had breathed on them and said, *"Receive ye the Holy Ghost" (John 20:22).* Nevertheless, the disciples had obedient hearts and even though they almost certainly did not fully understand the nature or necessity of the baptism they were about to receive, Jesus' word of command was quite enough for them.

Scripturally, it is clear that **all** true believers are indwelt with and sealed with the Holy Spirit.

*But ye are not in the flesh, but in the Spirit, if so be that the Spirit of God dwell in you.* **Now if any man have not the Spirit of Christ, he is none of his.** *(Romans 8:9)*

*In whom ye also trusted, after that ye heard the word of truth, the gospel of your salvation: in whom also **after that ye believed, ye were sealed with that holy Spirit of promise,*** (Ephesians 1:13)

However, there is a very wide difference between being indwelt and sealed with the Holy Spirit and being filled with the power of the Holy Spirit. The first takes place at our conversion and new birth. The second when we ask our Heavenly Father to fulfil His promise in believing faith.

*If ye then, being evil, know how to give good gifts unto your children: **how much more shall your heavenly Father give the Holy Spirit to them that ask him?*** (Luke 11:13)
(See chapter 4 for a fuller treatment of this verse to clear up some misunderstandings believers can have.)

Notice the number of times that this filling with the Holy Spirit is referred to by Jesus as a promise: *"the promise of my Father"* (Luke 24:49); *"the promise of the Father"* (Acts 1:4); *"received of the Father the promise of the Holy Ghost"* (Acts 2:33); *"For the promise is unto you"* (Acts 2:39).

So what was this promise for? We've previously seen that the Church already existed on the day of Pentecost. The Lord Jesus Christ gives a clear answer in the following verse:

*But ye shall receive power, after that the Holy Ghost is come upon you: **and ye shall be witnesses unto me** both in Jerusalem, and in all Judaea, and in Samaria, and unto the uttermost part of the earth.* (Acts 1:8)

We learn from this that, as far as the Lord Jesus Christ

was concerned, the enduing with power was to enable the disciples to become witnesses unto Him. Clearly He did not envisage the disciples (or, by extension, us) trying to be witnesses without this enduing with power from on high. Isn't this precisely the condition that most of the Western church is in? Could it be that the majority of believers in Britain have never been baptised with the Holy Spirit?

At this point some get hot under the collar and even feel insulted. But is this really the spiritual way to deal with a challenging question that might conflict with one's current understanding? Shouldn't we rather be like those Bereans, eager to receive the Word and prepared to search the Scriptures anew? Alas, how few seem to have a teachable spirit, thereby missing the promise and its blessing.

Once again we need to ask Dr Martyn Lloyd Jones' question to those who claim to have been baptised with the Holy Spirit when they were converted, namely, where is the evidence? Indeed, what evidence should we expect? As always, the best place to find an answer is in the Scriptures. We will look at the cases of our Lord Jesus Christ Himself, the Apostles, some early converts and finally the Apostle Paul. We will see a very interesting and instructive pattern emerging.

## THE LORD JESUS CHRIST

*Now the birth of Jesus Christ was on this wise: When as his mother Mary was espoused to Joseph, before they came together,* **she was found with child of the Holy Ghost.** *(Matthew 1:18)*
*But while he thought on these things, behold, the angel of the Lord appeared unto him in a dream, saying, Joseph, thou*

*son of David, fear not to take unto thee Mary thy wife: **for that which is conceived in her is of the Holy Ghost.** (Matthew 1:20)*

Notice that our Lord Jesus was born of the Holy Spirit from conception. However, we are not! If we are to be saved from our sins, we need to be "born again" of the Holy Spirit at some point after our natural birth. Let us notice that although the Lord Jesus was conceived and born of the Holy Spirit, He did not commence His earthly ministry until the Holy Spirit descended upon Him after He was baptised by John the Baptist in the Jordan.

*(Matthew 3:16) And Jesus, when he was baptized, went up straightway out of the water: and, lo, the heavens were opened unto him, and he saw the Spirit of God descending like a dove, and lighting upon him:*

*(Matthew 3:17) And lo a voice from heaven, saying, This is my beloved Son, in whom I am well pleased.*

In so many ways the Lord Jesus sets the pattern for His followers. Though He had no sin of which to repent, He underwent baptism in water after convincing John the Baptist that it was the right and proper thing to do. But why did He not commence His ministry until the Holy Spirit had descended upon Him?

Indeed as God the Son, He could have ministered (including the miraculous) in His own intrinsic power as God, yet He didn't. He waited until he had been baptised with the Holy Spirit. Surely the reason for this is that Jesus came to earth as a man, living and ministering in entire dependence upon God the Father. What He did, He did only as God the Holy Spirit enabled Him. In this way He is our representative Man and as His followers we are bidden to do likewise.

*Then said Jesus unto them, When ye have lifted up the Son of man, then shall ye know that I am he, **and that I do nothing of myself**; but as my Father hath taught me, I speak these things.  (John 8:28)*

Before leaving this look at our Saviour's life it would be profitable to review an incident in His life that occurred when He was twelve years old, long before the Holy Spirit came upon Him in the Jordan.

*(Luke 2:40)  And the child grew, and waxed strong in spirit, **filled with wisdom: and the grace of God was upon him.***
*(Luke 2:41)  Now his parents went to Jerusalem every year at the feast of the passover.*
*(Luke 2:42)  And when he was twelve years old, they went up to Jerusalem after the custom of the feast.*
*(Luke 2:43)  And when they had fulfilled the days, as they returned, the child Jesus tarried behind in Jerusalem; and Joseph and his mother knew not of it.*
*(Luke 2:44)  But they, supposing him to have been in the company, went a day's journey; and they sought him among their kinsfolk and acquaintance.*
*(Luke 2:45)  And when they found him not, they turned back again to Jerusalem, seeking him.*
*(Luke 2:46)  And it came to pass, that after three days they found him in the temple, sitting in the midst of the doctors, both hearing them, and asking them questions.*
*(Luke 2:47)  **And all that heard him were astonished at his understanding and answers.***

Surely this is a marvellous glimpse into His person, demonstrating clearly that His miraculous conception by the Holy Spirit had set Him apart from all others. However, our purpose here is to see whether a simple pattern emerges. We observe that, even before Jesus was baptised with the Holy Spirit at the Jordan, He was filled with wisdom and understanding and the grace of God was upon Him. This was clearly so evident that, *"all that heard him were astonished at his understanding and answers." (Luke 2:47)*

We might sum up the pattern as, firstly born of the Holy Spirit and later baptised or filled with the Holy Spirit. It is very clear that our Lord did not commence His ministry until He had received His baptism with the Holy Spirit. Every word of Scripture has something to teach us and the following verses are no exception.

*And **Jesus being full of the Holy Ghost** returned from Jordan, and was led by the Spirit into the wilderness, (Luke 4:1)*

Here we are not only told that Jesus returned from the Jordan, but that He was now FULL of the Holy Spirit. This is clearly a very important detail that we should not miss. It represented a watershed in His earthly life. Neither should we miss the first appointment God the Father had for His Son, now that He had been filled with the Holy Spirit.

*Then was Jesus led up of the Spirit into the wilderness **to be tempted of the devil**. (Matthew 4:1)*

In a very real sense His baptism with the Holy Spirit was the gateway into that realm which is the domain of the *"the prince of this world" (John 12:31)* and *"the prince of the power of the air" (Ephesians 2:2)*, namely Satan. An immediate conflict with the Devil was inevitable when our Saviour, who is *"the light of the world" (John 8:12)*, entered that province in which the battle is *"not against flesh and blood, but against principalities, against powers, against the rulers of the darkness of this world, against spiritual wickedness in high places."* (Ephesians 6:12).

Praise God we know the outcome of that terrible testing! Our Lord Jesus emerged from the wilderness victorious over the Devil. Before we leave His temptation, let us note a point of great importance to us. In the Devil's very first temptation of a hungry Jesus who had just been fasting for forty days, he tried to get Him to act upon His own initiative as the Son of God by turning a stone into bread. Jesus triumphed by refusing to act according to His own will, but instead wielded *"the sword of the Spirit, which is the word of God"* (Ephesians 6:17), thus submitting Himself in entire dependence upon God.

Isn't it at this very point that we too often fail? When we are brought into peculiarly trying circumstances, instead of waiting upon God for His deliverance, we yield to the temptation to try carnal means to get ourselves out of the difficulty. This robs us of an opportunity for glorifying God in the trial and demonstrating the reality of the Faith to an unbelieving world.

Now let us note how the Bible describes His return into Galilee to commence His ministry.

*And **Jesus returned in the power of the Spirit** into Galilee: and there went out a fame of him through all the region round about. (Luke 4:14)*

Again we need to notice *all* that this verse is telling us. The fact that *"Jesus returned in the power of the Spirit"* is a most important detail. It is the key to understanding by what means He conducted every aspect of His subsequent ministry. Namely, it was precisely in accordance with His Father's will and executed in the power of the Holy Spirit. As we have pointed out earlier, Jesus' ministry was most certainly not conducted according to His own initiative or using His own inherent power as God the Son.

Before we started to look for a pattern in this whole matter of being born of the Holy Spirit and subsequently baptised with the Holy Spirit, we asked what evidence one could expect to see in someone who was filled with the Holy Spirit. The first and highest example is of course the Lord Jesus Christ. However, we need to bear in mind what we are taught about Him in the following verse.

*For he whom God hath sent speaketh the words of God: for God giveth not the Spirit by measure unto him.* *(John 3:34)*

In other words there was no limitation to the fullness of the anointing that Christ received when the Holy Spirit descended upon Him in the Jordan. Although we are commanded to *"be filled with the Spirit" (Ephesians 5:18),* and will be if we seek God in faith, yet there is a limit to that precious filling. No one can claim to have received the Spirit without measure other than our Lord Jesus Christ. In that sense (and so many others) He is absolutely unique and stands apart from and above us all.

So, what effect did Jesus' early Spirit-filled ministry have upon His hearers? His sabbath day teaching at the synagogue in Nazareth created quite a stir! He had just been handed the book of the prophet Isaiah and began to read.

*(Luke 4:18)* **The Spirit of the Lord is upon me**, *because he hath anointed me to preach the gospel to the poor; he hath sent me to heal the brokenhearted, to preach deliverance to the captives, and recovering of sight to the blind, to set at liberty them that are bruised,*

*(Luke 4:19) To preach the acceptable year of the Lord.*

*(Luke 4:20) And he closed the book, and he gave it again to the minister, and sat down. And the eyes of all them that were in the synagogue were fastened on him.*

*(Luke 4:21) And he began to say unto them,* **This day is this scripture fulfilled in your ears**.

Here, in the plainest way possible, He was claiming to be the Messiah of Israel. To get a fuller understanding of the whole scene, please read Luke 4:16-30. The words Jesus read were from Isaiah 61:1 and the first half of verse 2. The wonderful thing is that these words were written about the Lord Jesus Christ seven centuries before His actual advent into this world. Note the very first words, *"The Spirit of the Lord is upon me"* and indeed the Spirit of the Lord *was* upon Him! What was their reaction?

They stumbled at His words because they thought of Him only as the 'local boy' whose father, Joseph the carpenter, they knew. Of course, they were ignorant of the fact that Jesus had no earthly father. This enabled Jesus to bring out the truth that, *"No prophet is accepted in his own country"* (Luke 4:24). Sadly this principle is still alive and well in the Church today. Too often if God gifts a man or a woman and especially if He baptises them with His Holy Spirit, it is neither believed, understood nor appreciated by their brethren. This usually results in a 'wilderness experience' for a season and it is not uncommon that the individual is forced to leave his or her church. Dear reader, if this should be your experience, although difficult and painful, praise the Lord for it because you will be in good company, i.e. His!

If you have read the whole passage you will know that the men of Nazareth were so incensed by our Lord's claim to be their Messiah that they led Him up to the brow of the hill on which their city was built with the intention of hurling Him down to His death. However, it was not His time and so *"he passing through the midst of them went his way" (Luke 4:30)*. Marvellous!

An interesting thought is this: what would have happened if Jesus had not been filled with the Holy Spirit and had stood up and read exactly the same words to them? Although we cannot know for certain, I believe they would probably have put it down to misguided enthusiasm or perhaps sunstroke or some such thing. He would have been told to sit down and that would probably have been the end of it. However, because He *was* filled with the Holy Spirit, His words were driven home to the hearts of His hearers with power. It was this that made all the difference.

Likewise today it is very common to hear preaching that is doctrinally correct (which is essential) but which is devoid of real power. It is painful to hear the Gospel preached by a man who is not full of the Holy Spirit. Someone once used the expression, "It's as dry as an old barn door!" Many of the preachers of yesteryear knew what it was to be filled with the Holy Spirit. They called it 'unction' and would have regarded it as the greatest of calamities to mount the pulpit without it.

## THE APOSTLES

So far it has been a joy to dwell on the supreme example of the Lord Jesus Christ Himself, but we must now move on to look at the case of the Apostles. We have already seen that they were born of the Holy Spirit on the same day that Jesus was raised from the dead. Thus they became the infant Church fifty days before Pentecost.

It is interesting to study what was going on amongst them during those fifty days. At one point Peter went back to his fishing accompanied by six of the disciples. After fishing all night and catching nothing (a good illustration of attempted soul winning for the Lord in our own strength) they see the risen Lord Jesus on the shoreline at daybreak. Upon following His instructions as to where to cast the net, they catch a miraculous draught of fish. Isn't this a wonderful picture of a toil worn Church, labouring for years in her own strength with little or nothing to show for it, but finally getting a revelation of her glorious risen Lord? Notice that this revelation was not produced by the disciples but came entirely at the Lord's initiative. The presence of the Lord, His Word of command (spoken in real-time into their situation) and their obedient response made all the difference. Might we respectfully say that it was not singing, church activity, Bible study or even 'good ministry' that turned the tide of their fortunes? These all have their place but are no substitute for the presence and power of the living God in our midst. If we are ever to realise why our assemblies are so barren in terms of soul winning, we need to have an encounter with the risen Lord Jesus Christ. This can only happen as we obediently submit to Him, asking Him to baptise us with His Holy Spirit. Yes, it is Jesus Himself who baptises us with the Holy Spirit. In the following verses John the Baptist sets forth this vital truth.

*(John 1:32) And John bare record, saying, I saw the Spirit descending from heaven like a dove, and it abode upon him.*

*(John 1:33) And I knew him not: but he that sent me to baptize with water, the same said unto me, Upon whom thou shalt see the Spirit descending, and remaining on him,* **the same is he which baptizeth with the Holy Ghost.**

*(John 1:34) And I saw, and bare record that* **this is the Son of God.**

In establishing our pattern by comparing the 'before and after' being baptised with the Holy Spirit it would be helpful to look at another aspect of what was going on among the disciples during those fifty days before Pentecost. The last ten days of that period are particularly interesting. They commenced when the Lord Jesus spoke to the disciples for the last time before ascending into heaven. As we saw earlier, He commanded them not to leave Jerusalem until they had received the promised power from above.

*And, being assembled together with them, commanded them that they should not depart from Jerusalem, but wait for the promise of the Father, which, saith he, ye have heard of me. (Acts 1:4)*

After seeing the Lord Jesus taken up into heaven, the disciples returned from the Mount of Olives to the upper room in Jerusalem. How did they occupy themselves during the ten day wait for the promise of the Father, the baptism with the Holy Spirit?

***These all continued with one accord in prayer and supplication,*** *with the women, and Mary the mother of Jesus, and with his brethren. (Acts 1:14)*

Clearly they spent the majority of the time in close fellowship and prayer. Two very important aspects of their fellowship are revealed in this verse, namely that they were *"with one accord"* and *"in prayer"*. In reading this verse it would be all too easy to miss the vital significance of these two details as a prelude to Pentecost.

Consider them being *"with one accord"*. This means much more than we might at first suppose. It means that they were perfectly united in heart, mind and judgement; there were no differences in doctrine between them; there would not have been some who believed in the baptism with the Holy Spirit and some who did not. Even in our more enlightened fellowships we are plagued with different views on this, that and the other teaching of the Word of God. Nevertheless, we see the infant Church here in an unleavened state. We had a brief look at the subject of leaven back in chapter 2, so please review that if you are not sure what we mean. Why was being *"with one accord"* so vitally important? Psalm 133 gives us the answer.

*(Psalms 133:1)  A Song of degrees of David.* ***Behold, how good and how pleasant it is for brethren to dwell together in unity!***
*(Psalms 133:2)  It is like* ***the precious ointment*** *upon the head, that ran down upon the beard, even Aaron's beard: that went down to the skirts of his garments;*
*(Psalms 133:3)  As* ***the dew*** *of Hermon, and as the dew that descended upon the mountains of Zion:* ***for there the LORD commanded the blessing****, even life for evermore.*

This short but beautiful psalm teaches that when we dwell together in *true* unity we can be sure that the Lord will command a blessing upon us; but what blessing in particular? The oil or ointment in verse 2 and the dew in verse 3 both typify the Holy Spirit poured out upon believers. What does true unity really mean though? First of all it is something which cannot be produced by man but comes from God alone. All the disciples were joined to the Lord Jesus Christ and to one another when He breathed the Holy Spirit into them on the day of His resurrection and the Church was born. More than that though, no leaven of false doctrine had got in among them and they all saw eye to eye. This was the first prerequisite for the wonderful fulfilment of God's promise at Pentecost. What was the other essential? We are told in that same verse that they continued with *"prayer and supplication" (Acts 1:14)*. Even though the Lord Jesus had told them that they would be baptised with the Holy Spirit, they still prayed for it and no doubt for other necessities also. They would have remembered the words of the Lord Jesus that we looked at earlier:

*If ye then, being evil, know how to give good gifts unto your children: how much more shall your heavenly Father give the Holy Spirit to them that **ask** him? (Luke 11:13)*
(See chapter 4 for a fuller treatment of this verse to clear up some misunderstandings believers can have.)

These words are clearly addressed to believers, since *only* they have a heavenly Father to ask in the first place. Neither can it be a prayer asking for salvation because we are not justified with God by asking for the Holy Spirit but by believing on the Lord Jesus Christ.

The principle of praying for something that God has promised in His Word is well supported in the Scriptures. For instance during the Babylonian captivity of the Jews, Daniel realised as he was reading the book of the prophet Jeremiah that God had determined that the length of their captivity would be seventy years. Far be it from Daniel to sit back at ease waiting for it to happen automatically, even though he realised that the prophesied time period was almost up.

*(Daniel 9:2) In the first year of his reign I Daniel understood by books the number of the years, whereof the word of the LORD came to Jeremiah the prophet, that he would accomplish seventy years in the desolations of Jerusalem.*

*(Daniel 9:3) And I set my face unto the Lord God, to seek by prayer and supplications, with fasting, and sackcloth, and ashes:*

It is well worth reading the agonised intercession of this godly man for the wayward people of God and the blessing that results. How many believers in Britain have recognised the desperate need of an outpouring of God's Holy Spirit upon themselves and the Church and have been moved to seek God about it in fervent prayer? We seem to have the view that repentance is only for the unbelievers outside of our 'holy huddles'. However, I firmly believe that God is looking for repentance in the Church over this whole matter of the Holy Spirit. We would do far better humbling ourselves under His mighty hand than rushing off to organise the next evangelistic outreach. Nowadays, even the greatest of these efforts in terms of man hours and financial input produce almost no fruit in terms of souls actually saved. When will we wake up to the real reason for this?

Bringing the focus back to the disciples in the upper room obediently waiting and praying for the promised enduing with power, how do our churches compare to them? Let us not forget that they were in that marvellous condition of being prayerful and with one accord before the Holy Spirit came upon them at Pentecost. Surely the truth is that we do not compare well. Many in the professing church are trying to create a visible unity by joining together with other local churches in the ecumenical or 'churches together' movement. The trouble with this is that it is a man-made 'unity' that necessarily compromises Truth as vital doctrine is supressed in order to accommodate others. Sadly, there is little doubt that the ecumenical movement is helping to produce the clearly prophesied apostate church of the last days. They will all gradually, but predictably, unify with the Church of Rome. We must remember that the Bible never instructs us to create unity. The unity between *true* believers already exists because it is created by God. We are told to try and *keep* the unity, not create it.

*Endeavouring to keep the unity of the Spirit in the bond of peace.  (Ephesians 4:3)*

Before we move on to look at the difference that the baptism with the Holy Spirit made to the disciples, this would be a good place to examine a stance taken by many cessationists (who do not believe in a separate baptism with the Holy Spirit). They will often make statements like, "When the Holy Spirit was given to the Church at Pentecost…" At first this sounds all well and good. The trouble is that this gives the impression that the Holy Spirit was given to the Church corporately, once and for all on that occasion. The teaching then follows, either explicitly or implicitly, that all believers since then have automatically received that baptism as if by proxy. Has anyone ever received water baptism by proxy?

If baptism with the Holy Spirit was by proxy, surely

the same logic could have been applied in our Lord Jesus' instructions to the disciples regarding the need to be baptised with the Holy Spirit. Instead of commanding them to wait in Jerusalem for the promised enduing with power from on high, He could have said something like this, "Since I as Head of the Church have already been filled with the Holy Spirit at the Jordan, you are all automatically filled by virtue of your union to Me. Now go into the world and preach the Gospel to every creature". Clearly, this is not what the Lord said! Each disciple received an individual filling with the Holy Spirit after waiting in faith and prayer for it. The same is true of the Apostle Paul and the early converts as we shall see later. The question our cessationist brothers need to answer is this: at what point in Church history did God alter this arrangement so that modern believers are endued with power from on high automatically at the point of their conversion?

We should reiterate at this point that all of this confusion arises from the mistaken idea that the Church was born on the day of Pentecost. To believe that leads inevitably to misunderstanding completely God's purpose in Pentecost. Surely it is a foundational error that has unnecessarily brought much mischief and weakness upon the modern Western Church.

We now need to take a close look at the difference that the baptism with the Holy Spirit made to the disciples.

*(Acts 2:1)  And when the day of Pentecost was fully come, **they were all with one accord** in one place.*
*(Acts 2:2)  And **suddenly** there came a sound from heaven as of a rushing mighty wind, and it filled all the house where they were sitting.*

*(Acts 2:3)  And there appeared unto them cloven tongues like as of fire, and it sat upon each of them.*

*(Acts 2:4)  And **they were all filled with the Holy Ghost**, and began to speak with other tongues, as the Spirit gave them utterance.*

First of all we are given another reminder of the quality of fellowship enjoyed by the disciples; *"they were all with one accord"*. We were previously told this vital bit of information in Acts 1:14, so we can be quite sure that God wants us to take note of this. In fact, the expression occurs several more times in the Book of Acts.

*Suddenly* it happened; the promise of the Father was fulfilled. How distasteful and vulgar many of us seem to regard the thought of God doing anything amongst us *suddenly*. We much prefer the thought that after years of patient Bible study, perhaps a course at a theological college and a few letters after our name and receiving the praise of men we might just, very gradually, be filled with the Holy Spirit. No no, this is not God's way. The baptism with the Holy Spirit is not an attainment that can be earned through human effort, but rather a doorway that introduces us into a sphere of service that can be entered in no other way. It is not a goal but a gateway. Just as our Lord Jesus described Himself as the door that we must enter through in order to be saved (John 10:9), so the baptism in the Holy Spirit is the entrance to the Spirit-filled life that God intends for *every* believer. It needs to be emphasised that being filled with the Holy Spirit is but a *beginning* of the Spirit-filled life. It is most certainly not instant maturity or immediate sanctification. These develop as the Word of God, the Holy Spirit, trials and testing all do their work in us.

So, what difference did this baptism make? The first effect of being filled with the Holy Spirit was a clearly supernatural manifestation. They were miraculously enabled to speak in languages that they had never learned. There was of course a distinct purpose in this. At that time there were thousands of Jews from many different nations, all gathered in Jerusalem for the annual feast of Pentecost. These all heard, in their own native tongue, the disciples speaking forth the wonderful works of God. The crowds were astounded. Nevertheless it is not primarily this result that I want to draw to your attention. Rather, it is the amazing boldness that the disciples now displayed, epitomised by Peter's masterly sermon in which, among other things, he charged them with having just crucified their own Messiah. Let us not forget that this is the same Peter who denied knowing his Lord only a few weeks previously! Humanly the disciples were putting themselves in great danger by confronting thousands of fellow Jews with their great national sin. Yet, filled with the Holy Spirit, the fear of man was totally eclipsed by a supreme trust and confidence in God. The Holy Spirit Himself was the source of that bold confidence and therefore He ensured that it was honoured with results that glorified God, namely regenerating 3000 souls and thus adding them to the Church.

We see then that the baptism with the Holy Spirit literally made *all* the difference to the disciples' ability to be witnesses to the Lord Jesus Christ. In Peter's sermon he proclaimed to those who would repent that they would likewise receive the promise of the Father, the gift of the Holy Spirit.

*Then Peter said unto them, Repent, and be baptized every one of you in the name of Jesus Christ for the remission of sins,* ***and ye shall receive the gift of the Holy Ghost. For the promise*** *is unto you, and to your children, and to all that are afar off, even as many as the Lord our God shall call.* (Acts 2:38-39)

We shouldn't move on from these verses without again drawing attention to the far reaching intention of God for His promise of an enduing with power. It was not just for the Apostles but for their hearers, their hearers' children, all that were 'afar off' and indeed as many as God would call. Thus we see clearly that God intended to make the gift of the Holy Spirit available to all believers throughout the Church Age.

## EARLY CONVERTS

Among the early converts, probably the clearest illustration of the pattern (first converted and subsequently filled with the Holy Spirit) is found in Acts chapter 8.

*(Acts 8:5)  Then Philip went down to the city of Samaria, and preached Christ unto them.*

*(Acts 8:6)  And the people with one accord gave heed unto those things which Philip spake, hearing and seeing the miracles which he did.*

*(Acts 8:7)  For unclean spirits, crying with loud voice, came out of many that were possessed with them: and many taken with palsies, and that were lame, were healed.*

*(Acts 8:8)  And there was great joy in that city.*

*(Acts 8:9)  But there was a certain man, called Simon, which beforetime in the same city used sorcery, and bewitched the people of Samaria, giving out that himself was some great one:*

*(Acts 8:10)  To whom they all gave heed, from the least to the greatest, saying, This man is the great power of God.*

*(Acts 8:11)  And to him they had regard, because that of long time he had bewitched them with sorceries.*

*(Acts 8:12)* **But when they believed Philip preaching the things concerning the kingdom of God, and the name of Jesus Christ, they were baptized, both men and women.**

*(Acts 8:13) Then Simon himself believed also: and when he was baptized, he continued with Philip, and wondered, beholding the miracles and signs which were done.*

*(Acts 8:14) Now when the apostles which were at Jerusalem heard that Samaria had received the word of God, they sent unto them Peter and John:*

*(Acts 8:15) Who, when they were come down, prayed for them, that they might receive the Holy Ghost:*

*(Acts 8:16) (For as yet he was fallen upon none of them: only they were baptized in the name of the Lord Jesus.)*

*(Acts 8:17)* **Then laid they their hands on them, and they received the Holy Ghost.**

*(Acts 8:18) And when Simon **saw** that through laying on of the apostles' hands the Holy Ghost was given, he offered them money*

This really is a most interesting passage. Leaving aside the extraordinary case of the man called Simon, we see here the conversion of a large number of men and women under the preaching of Philip in Samaria. It would be too easy to gloss over the details that are given to us without noticing something very important. In verse 12 we read of the conversion and subsequent baptism in water of these Samaritan people. Clearly, they were saved at that point. If any of them had died just afterwards they would have gone to Heaven.

As we have now pointed out many times, much of our modern evangelical doctrine would say that these believers must have been baptised with the Holy Spirit at the point of their conversion. However, we now see something very interesting. Samaria was more than thirty miles from Jerusalem. This doesn't seem far by today's standards, but in the first century news only travelled as fast as walking or perhaps horseback. Being realistic, would someone have been dispatched to Jerusalem immediately after these conversions? It's possible, but we just don't know. Once the news had reached the Apostles in Jerusalem, there must have been a further lapse of time whilst they deliberated and made a decision to send Peter and John to Samaria. There would then have been the journey time to Samaria. It is therefore reasonable to assume that the interval between the Samaritans' conversion and the arrival of the Apostles would have been at least days and possibly even weeks. The important point to grasp here is that there was a *significant* interval.

Now let us notice what it was that the Apostles considered so important that they must travel up to Samaria. Surely if the doctrine that modern cessationists teach is correct, then the Apostles needn't have bothered themselves. They would have just assumed that the Samaritans had been baptised with the Holy Spirit at the point of their conversion. Nevertheless, they knew from Jesus' teaching and their own experience that there was a difference between being 'born again' at conversion and subsequently being filled or baptised with the Holy Spirit. Fresh in their minds would be the fact that Jesus had commanded them to wait in Jerusalem until they were filled with the Holy Spirit at Pentecost. It was not a suggestion or an 'optional extra' for the Christian. The Apostles understood that, without this baptism, the new believers at Samaria would not be equipped to fulfil Christ's great commission of taking the Gospel into a hostile world.

Once Peter and John had arrived in Samaria, we are told in verses 15 to 17 that they prayed for the new believers to receive the Holy Spirit. The apostles then laid their hands on the new converts and they were baptised with the Holy Spirit. Again, leaving aside the interesting case of Simon himself, let us notice in verse 18 that he *saw* that through the laying on of the Apostles' hands, the Holy Spirit was given. In other words, there was a very obvious manifestation of the reality of this baptism.

Dear reader, do you see that yet again the pattern of first converted and later filled with the Holy Spirit is repeated with these Samaritan believers? Again we ask the question, where in the Scriptures are we told that this is no longer the case and that you now 'get it all at conversion'?

Perhaps here, before moving on to demonstrate the same pattern in the case of the Apostle Paul, it would be timely to mention one instance in which the baptism with the Holy Spirit appears to have been given almost simultaneously with conversion. This is the case of Cornelius and his household in Acts chapter 10. This demonstrates that the filling with the Holy Spirit *can* occur at the time of conversion, but it is not the norm. Importantly, the account makes very clear that there was a plainly discernible manifestation of the Holy Spirit in those new believers.

*(Acts 10:44) While Peter yet spake these words, the Holy Ghost fell on all them which heard the word.*
*(Acts 10:45) And they of the circumcision which believed were astonished, as many as came with Peter, because that on the Gentiles also was poured out the gift of the Holy Ghost.*
*(Acts 10:46a)* **For they heard them speak with tongues, and magnify God.**

Some have attempted to evade the implication that a manifestation such as tongues or prophesying should occur when believers are baptised with the Holy Spirit. They have emphasised the need of the Jewish contingent accompanying Peter to see a particularly convincing demonstration that God was including the Gentiles in the Church. Doubtless this was true, however the Scriptures are silent as to whether that was the *only* reason that Cornelius and his household spoke in tongues and magnified God. Also, Peter had previously gone up to Samaria with John (Acts chapter 8) for the express purpose of ensuring that the new believers there received the filling of the Holy Spirit. The Samaritans were second only to the Gentiles in terms of being despised by the Jews, yet the Apostles had no difficulty in believing the reports of their conversion before going there. Therefore when the Samaritans gave clear manifestations (which Simon *saw*) after being filled with the Holy Spirit, these were certainly not needed in order to convince Peter and John that God had included them in the Church.

## THE APOSTLE PAUL

To finish off this chapter we will take a look at the case of the Apostle Paul to see if we can establish the same pattern as we have now seen several times.

*(Acts 9:1) And Saul, yet breathing out threatenings and slaughter against the disciples of the Lord, went unto the high priest,*

*(Acts 9:2) And desired of him letters to Damascus to the synagogues, that if he found any of this way, whether they were men or women, he might bring them bound unto Jerusalem.*

*(Acts 9:3) And as he journeyed, he came near Damascus:*

*and suddenly there shined round about him a light from heaven:*

*(Acts 9:4) And he fell to the earth, and heard a voice saying unto him, Saul, Saul, why persecutest thou me?*

*(Acts 9:5) And he said, Who art thou, **Lord**? And the Lord said, I am Jesus whom thou persecutest: it is hard for thee to kick against the pricks.*

*(Acts 9:6) And he trembling and astonished said, **Lord, what wilt thou have me to do?** And the Lord said unto him, **Arise**, and go into the city, and it shall be told thee what thou must do.*

The above well-known passage describes the conversion of the Apostle Paul. If he is to conform to the pattern that we have already seen, we need to see an interval between his conversion and subsequent filling with the Holy Spirit. Do we find this?

*And he was **three days** without sight, and neither did eat nor drink. (Acts 9:9)*

During those three days the Lord was convincing a disciple named Ananias to go to Saul. What happened when Ananias obeyed this command?

*(Acts 9:17) And Ananias went his way, and entered into the house; and putting his hands on him said, Brother Saul, the Lord, even Jesus, that appeared unto thee in the way as thou camest, hath sent me, that thou mightest receive thy sight, **and be filled with the Holy Ghost.***

*(Acts 9:18) And **immediately** there fell from his eyes as it had been scales: and he received sight forthwith, and arose, and was baptized.*

So, here we have it again. We see that three days elapsed between Saul's conversion and his being filled with the Holy Spirit. Note that word *"immediately"* in verse 18. Whilst there are many things that God might constrain us to wait a long time for, there are times when He acts *immediately.* How much do we know of God's sudden or immediate actions in our fellowships? Verse 18 also shows that Paul was baptised in water after he was filled with the Holy Spirit. This order is not always the same, as we saw with the Samaritan believers; they had been baptised in water before the Apostles arrived from Jerusalem to pray for and lay their hands on them that they might be filled with the Holy Spirit.

Let us also notice that Ananias was not an apostle and yet the Lord was perfectly able to use him to impart the gift of the Holy Spirit to Paul. This clearly demonstrates that the laying on of hands to impart this gift was not the sole prerogative of the Apostles. In fact the laying on of hands was not always needed as we saw in the case of the Roman centurion, Cornelius, in Acts chapter 10.

## CONCLUSION

We started this chapter with the intention of showing God's purpose, as far as the Church is concerned, in Pentecost. We have seen that the baptism with the Holy Spirit is not automatic upon conversion and that there is almost always a significant interval between the two events. To demonstrate this we looked at the cases of the Lord Jesus Christ Himself, the disciples, the Samaritan converts and the Apostle Paul. Dear reader can you see that because of the popular modern teaching that 'you get it all at conversion', the post conversion interval for many saints lasts for their entire Christian lives?

This answers the question as to whether you can be a truly born-again believer and yet never have been baptised with the Holy Spirit. The answer from all the foregoing examples is clearly yes! Nevertheless, it is also clear from these same examples that it is not God's purpose that a believer should remain in that condition. Saved they most certainly are, but what will be the reckoning of their service without that equipping which God clearly considers essential?

# CHAPTER 4

# ASK, SEEK, KNOCK

In chapter 1 we mentioned Brother Yun and his impression of the Western Church after he finally escaped from China. As a new believer he longed to have a copy of the Bible, but it was illegal and very risky to own one. In answer to Yun's fervent prayers, God got a Bible into his hands by the most extraordinary means. What happened could have come straight from the pages of the Book of Acts. So many of us Western Christians, who rarely (if ever) experience God moving in such marvellous ways, dearly need to read such accounts to awaken us.

As he read his precious Bible, Brother Yun came across this verse:

*But ye shall receive power, after that the Holy Ghost is come upon you: and ye shall be witnesses unto me both in Jerusalem, and in all Judaea, and in Samaria, and unto the uttermost part of the earth.* (Acts 1:8)

He was not sure who the Holy Spirit was, so he ran to ask his mother. She was illiterate and knew only a few verses from the Bible that she had learned from other believers. Yet the simple answer she gave displayed a wonderful, God-given wisdom.

*"I've already told you all I can remember. Why don't you pray and **ask** God for the Holy Spirit just like you prayed for your Bible?"*

Yun took his mother's advice and prayed the following:

*"I need the power of the Holy Spirit. I am willing to be your witness."*

Brother Yun then described what happened:

*"After the prayer God's spirit of joy fell upon me. A deep revelation of God's love and presence flooded my being. I'd never enjoyed singing before but many new songs of worship flowed from my lips. They were words I had never learned before. Later I wrote them down. The songs are still sung in the Chinese house churches to this day."*

If your heart has been stirred and warmed by all that you have read so far, then praise God! You may be well on your way to receiving the baptism with the Holy Spirit. The mnemonic ASK, standing for 'Ask, Seek, Knock,' might be helpful to you as you wait upon God in prayer.

*(Luke 11:9) And I say unto you, **Ask**, and it shall be given you; **seek**, and ye shall find; **knock**, and it shall be opened unto you.*

*(Luke 11:10) For every one that **asketh** receiveth; and he that **seeketh** findeth; and to him that **knocketh** it shall be opened.*

These wonderful words from the lips of our Lord Jesus Christ assure us of success in petitioning our heavenly Father concerning one of His promises to us. However, we would be wise to note what else Jesus said in this particular discourse to enable us to check our heart's motive in the matter.

The subject of this section in Luke chapter 11 is prayer. The Lord had just been praying and, when He had finished, one of the disciples asked Him to teach them to pray. His answer is recorded from verse 2 through to verse 13. The section up until verse 4 is what is commonly called, 'The Lord's Prayer' but which should more accurately be called, 'The Disciples' Prayer'. Nevertheless, it is what follows that we need to take a close look at.

*(Luke 11:5)  And he said unto them, Which of you shall have a friend, and shall go unto him at midnight, and say unto him, Friend, lend me three loaves;*
*(Luke 11:6)  For a friend of mine in his journey is come to me, and I have nothing to set before him?*
*(Luke 11:7)  And he from within shall answer and say, Trouble me not: the door is now shut, and my children are with me in bed; I cannot rise and give thee.*
*(Luke 11:8)  I say unto you, Though he will not rise and give him, because he is his friend, yet because of his importunity he will rise and give him as many as he needeth.*
*(Luke 11:9)  And I say unto you, Ask, and it shall be given you; seek, and ye shall find; knock, and it shall be opened unto you.*
*(Luke 11:10)  For every one that asketh receiveth; and he that seeketh findeth; and to him that knocketh it shall be opened.*

Some commentaries concentrate on the very valid teaching of this illustration regarding encouragement to pray. They rightly make the point that it does not teach that God is annoyed with our prayers, or in any way unwilling to answer them. On the contrary, in contrast with the man who was at first unwilling to get out of his bed, God is so much more willing to hear and answer our prayers. This is further illustrated in verses 11 to 13, which we will look at shortly.

The aspect that I want to draw to your attention however is the matter of motive. The man who goes to a friend's house at midnight asking for three loaves is not motivated by his own need, but by the need of another friend who, in his travels, has arrived unannounced at a late hour in need of hospitality. Realising that his own cupboards are bare, he hastens to his neighbour's house, not put off by the lateness of the hour. Clearly he also has good reason to believe that the neighbour will have an ample supply of bread.

Are we warranted in considering this scenario in a spiritual sense? I believe that we are, because our Lord concludes His teaching on the whole matter in verse 13, where He makes the subject of the prayer the Holy Spirit. We will shortly look more closely at the whole matter of believers, who necessarily already *have* the Holy Spirit in one sense, asking for the Holy Spirit in the sense of verse 13.

Imagine a friend in great need calling upon you for help. They may or may not be a believer, but in either case have some peculiarly difficult issue requiring your help. Upon honest reflection, you realise your own inadequacy in terms of spiritual discernment and equipping. You have heard other Christians testify about the baptism with the Holy Spirit and the spiritual gifts that He bestows at His sovereign discretion. Perhaps one of these gifts might provide the very key needed to unlock the metaphorical prison cell keeping your friend captive. However, you attend an assembly that teaches that

God withdrew all of the supernatural gifts of the Holy Spirit once the New Testament Scriptures were completed. Clearly, if this teaching was true it would be absolutely pointless going to God in prayer and asking Him to fill you with His Holy Spirit and equip you with any spiritual gifts that He considered necessary.

So you now have a choice. You could give that spare copy of the New Testament and Psalms on your bookshelf to your friend with a recommended reading plan, wish them well and send them on their way. Or you could be like one of the noble Bereans; you could determine to search the Scriptures afresh, asking, seeking and knocking at the door of God in prayer, with the request that He would show you whether or not your assembly's teaching on this vital matter is correct. Upon finding that the Scriptures do not support that teaching, you would be free to wait upon God in prayer in the full expectation that He would baptise you with the Holy Spirit and gift you according to His will. Of course it would have been even better had you already been full of the Holy Spirit and equipped to help your friend!

In the scenario just described, can you see a spiritual re-enactment of the illustration that the Lord Jesus gives us in Luke 11:5-10? You have a friend who needs profound spiritual help but you are conscious that your 'spiritual cupboards' are bare as far as having precisely what this friend needs. Pride might tempt you to pretend that you were already suitably equipped. However, assuming that that temptation has been resisted, in the same way that the man went to knock on his friend's door for bread at midnight, you must knock on God's door by prayer asking for all that you need in order to help your friend. We know that God is well pleased with such prayers because they are motivated by love and concern for others and are not self-centred. If our motivation in praying for the filling with the Holy Spirit is also genuine concern for God's glory and the honour of His Name, so much the better.

It is clear from Paul's first letter to the Corinthians, chapters 12, 13 and 14, that the gifts of the Holy Spirit should primarily be used for the edification and building up of the Church. Nevertheless, there are times when certain gifts might be used in our dealings with those who are not yet saved.

*(1 Corinthians 14:24)  But if **an unbeliever** or an inquirer comes in while everyone is prophesying, they are **convicted of sin** and are brought under judgment by all,*
*(1 Corinthians 14:25)  as the secrets of their hearts are laid bare. So they will fall down and worship God, exclaiming, "God is really among you!"*

In his book "Gathering the Faithful Remnant", Philip Powell cites some very instructive and challenging instances of this in Church history. The following are some quotes from his book (pp. 391-394).

*"**Charles Haddon Spurgeon (1834-92)** was the prominent Baptist preacher in England during the 19th century, who spoke of a sermon at Exeter Hall in which he suddenly broke off from his subject, and pointing in a certain direction, said, 'Young man, those gloves you are wearing have not been paid for: you have stolen them from your employer'. At the close of the service, a young man, looking very pale and greatly agitated, came to the room, which was used as a vestry, and begged for a private interview with Spurgeon. On being admitted, he placed a pair of gloves upon the table, and tearfully said, 'It's the first time I*

*have robbed my master, and I will never do it again. You won't expose me, sir, will you? It would kill my mother if she heard that I had become a thief."*

*"On another occasion while he was preaching, Spurgeon said there was a man in the gallery who had a bottle of gin in his pocket. This not only startled the man in the gallery who had the gin, but it also led to his conversion."*

There were many more such incidences in the ministry of C H Spurgeon. On one occasion, whilst preaching, he pointed to a man sat in the midst of the crowd and declared him to be a shoemaker who kept his shop open on Sundays. He further declared how much money the man had taken the previous Sunday and what portion of that was profit! Clearly, this was a divinely given revelation to Spurgeon who had no knowledge of his own about the man. This use of a gift of the Holy Spirit led to the shoemaker's conversion.

*"**Os Guinness**: 'Speaking once at Essex University, I saw sitting in the front row a strange-looking girl with an odd expression on her face. Remembering an incident the previous night when a radical had tried to disrupt the lecture, I spoke on but also prayed silently that she would create no trouble. She remained quiet the whole evening but came up as soon as it was finished with a very troubled look and asked me what spell I had cast to keep her quiet. She told me she was part of a spiritist circle in the south of England and that the spirits had ordered her to travel to Essex, where she had never been before, to disrupt a series of lectures beginning that week. The curious sequel to this was that when I arrived back in Switzerland someone else in the community, far from a fanciful visionary, asked me what had happened in the Essex lectures. Praying*

*for them one morning, she had seen a vision, as real as waking reality, the lecture hall and the strange girl about to disrupt the meeting. Having prayed for her, she was convinced that nothing had happened, but she wondered if it was just her imagination. The presence of a Christian praying in the power of the Holy Spirit is always enough to render the occult inoperable.' "*

This incident related by Os Guinness is instructive in demonstrating the reality of Satanic opposition to meetings in which the Holy Spirit is *really* at work. Many Christians reading such accounts experience a sort of 'disconnect' from what they are reading because it falls completely outside the sphere of their own experience. "Nothing like this ever happens in our meetings" they would say. Perhaps the reason for this is that their own meeting is one in which the Holy Spirit is 'institutionally quenched' by cessationist teaching or a prevailing and overbearing human control. The Devil doubtless has little to fear from such meetings and therefore concentrates his efforts against congregations where the Holy Spirit is unhindered in His operations. However, the lesson to take away from this is that God is easily able to render Satan's attacks ineffective in response to prayer. Notice also that it was God who took the initiative in giving a vision to a spiritually receptive believer in Switzerland, prompting her to pray in the first place.

Clearly these examples (and there are many more) would cause a strict cessationist a lot of problems. Yet here they are, coming from the most reliable of sources. How much better to be willing to examine cessationist dogma in the light of the Scriptures, rather than trying to explain away well-documented instances of the Holy Spirit's gifts at work.

Whilst we are dealing with gifts of the Holy Spirit as they might have a bearing on our dealings with non-Christians, I believe it would be helpful to recount a case known to the author. The following regrettable incident would perhaps come under the heading of 'missed opportunities'.

A distressed woman telephoned a Brethren Assembly and spoke to one of the elders who listened carefully to her story. It transpired that she was experiencing frightening occult phenomena in her house in the form of objects being thrown about at random. Apparently she had recently moved into the house with her children but the experiences, commonly attributed to a poltergeist, had followed her from her previous residence. A Spirit-filled Christian should have an enhanced awareness of the reality of the supernatural realm, the existence of demons and their malignant activities. The Scriptures bear abundant testimony to the reality of this. However, the woman's account was received with a considerable degree of scepticism and unbelief. Nevertheless, the elder and his wife agreed to go to the woman's house with her to see for themselves. They were not expecting to witness anything and indeed they did not. It is difficult to know for certain why there were no manifestations for them to witness, but I believe the most likely explanation is this: God in His mercy knew that they were ill-equipped to confront such a situation and moved to protect them by restraining the ability of the demon or demons to act whilst they were present. I understand that the elder and his wife concluded that the woman's problem was more likely to be an overactive imagination. Whether the opportunity was taken to present the Gospel at any point in the proceedings, I don't know. Even if it had, would it be likely to have had much impact now that the woman had witnessed the general scepticism and apparent lack of any

Christian answer to her problem? Just as a reminder, this Brethren Assembly in common with virtually all others would have been cessationist in its outlook, meaning that the vast majority of the believers there would not have been baptised with the Holy Spirit and would therefore possess none of His supernatural gifts.

Had the tormented woman contacted a fellowship where there were some experienced, Spirit-filled believers, the outcome might have been very different. Firstly, she would have been listened to by somebody who understood the reality of these things and could explain to her what was probably going on. Secondly, she would have been quizzed as to whether she had been involved in séances, spiritist meetings, fortune telling or similar occult activities. That would also provide an open door to explain the Gospel, with the possibility of her repenting of her sin, coming to faith in the Lord Jesus Christ and being freed from demonic interference in her life. Thirdly, the fellowship would have prayed, seeking the Lord's guidance on whether to go to the house or not. If they felt that the house should be visited then at least two men, known to be full of the Holy Spirit and preferably to have had some experience in dealing with the demonic, would be sent.

However, we must now return to a verse that we said we would examine more closely earlier in this chapter.

*If ye then, being evil, know how to give good gifts unto your children: how much more shall your heavenly Father give the Holy Spirit to them that ask him? (Luke 11:13)*

It is important that we do not lose sight of the context in which these words of the Lord Jesus are set. They are the culmination of His teaching on prayer to the disciples, after one of them had asked him saying, *"Lord, teach us to pray, as John also taught his disciples." (Luke 11:1)* We are all very familiar with the first part of His answer, which is known as the Lord's Prayer. However, we need to understand His teaching on prayer as a whole. In dealing with this verse J. G. Bellet, an early Brethren writer, wrote:

*"It is significant that the gift He selects as the one we most need, and the one He most desires to give, is the Holy Spirit."*

This teaching of the Lord Jesus has caused difficulty to many believers. The reason for this is that it is clear from other Scriptures that *all* true believers are indwelt and sealed with the Person of the Holy Spirit.

*But ye are not in the flesh, but in the Spirit, if so be that the Spirit of God dwell in you.* **Now if any man have not the Spirit of Christ, he is none of his.** *(Romans 8:9)*

*In whom ye also trusted, after that ye heard the word of truth, the gospel of your salvation: in whom also **after that ye believed, ye were sealed with that holy Spirit of promise**, (Ephesians 1:13)*

So how can we reconcile the apparent contradiction in exhorting believers, who necessarily already have the Holy Spirit, to pray to their heavenly Father asking for the Holy Spirit? The Believer's Bible Commentary offers the following explanation:

*In the original Greek, verse 13 does not say that God will give the Holy Spirit, but rather He will "give Holy Spirit" (without the article). Professor H. B. Swete pointed out that when the article is present, it refers to the Person Himself, but when the article is absent, it refers to His gifts or operations on our behalf. So in this passage, it is not so much a prayer for the Person of the Holy Spirit, but rather for His ministries in our lives. This is further borne out by the parallel passage in Matthew 7:11 which reads, " ... how much more will your Father who is in heaven give good things to those who ask Him!"*

I believe that this helps to shed some light on the matter. Let us remind ourselves that the disciples had already received the Holy Spirit in the evening of the day of our Lord's resurrection (John 20:22). Yet forty days later the Lord Jesus commanded them to wait in Jerusalem until they were endued with power from on high when the Holy Spirit came upon them. Can anyone imagine that the Lord Jesus Christ Himself was not indwelt with the Holy Spirit (His human body having been conceived in Mary's womb by the overshadowing of the Holy Spirit) prior to that moment in the River Jordan when the Holy Spirit descended upon Him? Neither He nor His disciples commenced their respective ministries until after the Holy Spirit had descended upon them.

Humanly speaking, these things can seem difficult to understand. However, by comparing Scripture with Scripture we have to conclude that God is telling us that it is possible to be indwelt with the Holy Spirit and yet not empowered by the same Holy Spirit. In the wisdom of God, He has not made this enduing with power automatic upon conversion. Rather He has constrained us to exercise faith in His promise and pray to Him, asking Him to baptise or fill us with His Holy Spirit. As we said in the previous chapter, the disciples would doubtless have been praying for the fulfilment of the

Lord Jesus' last words to them as they waited on God during the ten days between His Ascension and Pentecost.

Some commentaries written by cessationists have had to acknowledge the difficulty presented by Luke 11:13. However, they tend to suggest that it is just an encouragement to pray that the Holy Spirit would produce His fruit (Galatians 5:22-23) in our lives. Doubtless we very much need this, but there is usually silence as regards being filled with a supernatural boldness to witness and receiving one or more of the gifts of the Holy Spirit listed in 1 Corinthians 12:8-10. This is only to be expected if they are to be consistent with their view that such obviously supernatural manifestations were withdrawn by God once the Canon of Scripture was completed. This view cannot be substantiated from the Scriptures alone and conflicts with well-documented evidence from Church history. If we are to be truly scriptural we cannot speak about the fruit of the Holy Spirit to the exclusion of the gifts of the Holy Spirit nor speak about the gifts to the exclusion of the fruit. Both are necessary in the Church.

In helping us to understand some of these principles, an analogy can sometimes be of assistance. Of course, analogies have their limitations and should not be pushed too far. To help understand how one can be indwelt with the Holy Spirit but not empowered, consider the case of a house. It is one thing to have electrical wiring installed, but on its own there will be none of the manifestations of electricity such as light, heat and sound etc. One has to ASK the electric company to turn on the power to your home. It would be quite futile to ask for the power to be turned on if one's home was not yet wired. However, once the power is laid on to a correctly wired house, it can be used under the control of the house owner; the lights do not come on and off at random but only as they are switched on or off. In a similar way, the gifts of the Holy Spirit are subject to the believer; someone with the gift of prophecy is not compelled to speak out a prophetic word the moment God gives one to him or her.

*And the spirits of the prophets are subject to the prophets.* (1 Corinthians 14:32)

Of course, we must be careful not to infer that the Holy Spirit is like electricity. The Holy Spirit is a divine Person, not a force or influence or any such thing.

It is interesting how prone we are to confuse and confound scriptural principles that differ. How few there were in Israel that understood that the only solution to the seemingly contradictory prophecies concerning their Messiah, was that the same Messiah would have two separate advents. Failure to realise this led the majority to reject their true Messiah. Similarly, many Christians confuse the Rapture of the Church with the Second Advent of the Lord Jesus Christ. Again, the Scriptures describing each of these events are very different in character and yet they get muddled and confused. This leads many believers to have their eyes looking down, focused on events here on Earth, rather than looking up with the joyful expectation of the imminent appearing of the Lord Jesus Christ in the clouds to catch away His Church before the Tribulation begins. Perhaps then, it is not surprising that there is so much confusion over the difference between being indwelt with the Holy Spirit at conversion and being 'clothed upon' with power as we are baptised with the Holy Spirit. A 'surgeon's scalpel' is surely needed in order to "rightly divide the word of truth".

We commenced this chapter with an exhortation to Ask, Seek and Knock with the assurance from our Saviour that we shall not do this in vain. There might be unbelief and many years of wrong teaching to overcome but, if we are willing, the Lord is able.

CHAPTER 5

# ILLUSTRATIONS FROM ISRAEL'S HISTORY

We must not take our doctrine from 'types and shadows' in the Old Testament. Nevertheless, we are warranted to look for and expect to find striking pictures of Truths clearly established in the New Testament as we diligently examine God's dealings with Israel in the Old Testament. This principle is taught in two of Paul's epistles.

*For whatsoever things were **written aforetime** were written **for our learning**, that we through patience and comfort of the scriptures might have hope.  (Romans 15:4)*

*Now all these things **happened unto them** (the Israelites) for ensamples (examples): and they are **written for our admonition**, upon whom the ends of the world are come.*
*(1 Corinthians 10:11)*

The things *"written aforetime"* refer to what we now call the Old Testament. Is it not sad when we hear of Christians who do not even read the Old Testament? It is quite impossible to have an intelligent understanding of the New Testament without knowing something of what has gone before. The following words of our Lord Jesus Christ are a warning to those inclined to ignore or disbelieve the Old Testament.

*(John 5:46) For had ye believed Moses, ye would have believed me: for he wrote of me.*

*(John 5:47) But if ye believe not his writings, how shall ye believe my words?*

By Moses' writings, our Lord meant the first five books of the Old Testament or Pentateuch. This of course includes the Genesis account of creation and Noah's flood. Our Lord's words to the Jewish religious hierarchy are also a salutary warning to today's professing Christians who have embraced the modern delusion of evolution. However, it is the history of God's dealings with Israel to which we will look to see if there are any aspects that foreshadow key truths revealed in the New Testament, but especially the truth of the baptism with the Holy Spirit.

## ESCAPING EGYPT THROUGH THE RED SEA

Surely the best-known Old Testament 'type' is that of God's wonderful deliverance of His people Israel from long and hard bondage in the nation of Egypt. By the hand of Moses, He led them miraculously through the Red Sea to freedom from Egypt and Pharaoh's tyranny. Many readers will be aware that in this literal history of Israel's deliverance, there is also a graphic illustration of the salvation of sinners through faith in the Lord Jesus Christ. Egypt represents the world and its ways; Pharaoh represents the Devil and his cruel reign over unsaved men and women; Moses is a 'type' of Christ who delivers those who trust in and follow Him from sin, Satan and the ungodly world-system.

So are there any examples that foreshadow the baptism

with the Holy Spirit as a separate and distinct matter from salvation? Well, there are a number that paint a fascinating picture if one looks beyond the literal history and immediate application to the children of Israel and sees a spiritual parallel in Christian experience. Perhaps the best place to start would be the continuing story of the Israelites after they had been safely delivered from Egypt.

## ENTERING CANAAN THROUGH THE RIVER JORDAN

The journey by foot from Mount Sinai to Kadesh Barnea on the threshold of the Promised Land could have been completed in only eleven days (see Deuteronomy 1:2). Nevertheless, because of Israel's unbelief and disobedience it actually took forty years. God determined that none of that generation, except Joshua and Caleb, would enter the Promised Land. Much could be said and many valuable lessons for the Church learned from those years of wilderness wandering. However, it is their eventual entry into the Promised Land that we are going to examine.

We have already noted the parallel between Israel's deliverance from Egypt and Pharaoh's dominion and the liberation of sinners from the world, sin and Satan's power. It is not difficult to see the symbolic significance of the Red Sea crossing as representing baptism by immersion in water for those who have put their faith in Jesus Christ for salvation. Now when God's people were finally ready to enter the Promised Land, there was another stretch of water barring the way, namely the River Jordan. Preachers have often used the Jordan as a 'type' of death, which believers must cross in order to arrive in Heaven on the other side. A line in the well-known hymn "Thine be the Glory" expresses this understanding: "… *bring us safe through Jordan to thy home above.*" Whilst this concept might help us to see that, for believers, death is but a river to be forded, it necessarily makes the land of Canaan (i.e. the Promised Land) to be a 'type' of Heaven. The problem with this is that in Canaan there were giants and many other enemies to be overcome, whereas in Heaven there will be no more warfare but rather endless joy, peace and bliss in the glorious presence of our Lord and Saviour, Jesus Christ. Not only that, but the Jews were eventually carried away from the land as captives by the Babylonians of which there will be no parallel for those in Heaven. Therefore Canaan cannot accurately be seen as symbolic of Heaven.

If the Promised Land is not a 'type' of Heaven, what could it represent in Christian experience? Clearly, in Israel's redemptive journey from Egypt, through the Red Sea, via a very circuitous wilderness route to the River Jordan, Canaan was the place that God would have his redeemed people to occupy. It was promised to them by covenant and all they had to do was believe God and in so doing march forwards to possess the land. Of course we know that, because of their unbelief, things were not as straightforward as that. Although sanctioned by God, there was the matter of the twelve spies being sent into the land. The adverse, faithless report of ten of them was enough to strike fear into the hearts of the whole host, despite the good and faithful testimony of Joshua and Caleb. When later, under Joshua's leadership, they were on the threshold of Canaan, only the River Jordan stood between them and the land. Just as He had done previously with the Red Sea, God now miraculously parted the waters of the Jordan so that His people could pass safely through. Thus the Jordan, which symbolises another baptism, became a gateway for the people to pass through into their promised inheritance. Notice that the Jordan was not a goal for the people, but a gateway.

Dear reader, can you see the remarkable parallels in all of this to the promised baptism with the Holy Spirit for believers? For Christians the equivalent of the 'Promised Land' would be the Spirit-filled life that can only be entered when one is filled or baptised with the Holy Spirit for the first time. Again, this baptism is a gateway (not a goal) into a sphere of Christian experience and service that cannot be entered into any other way. Overleaf is a table to help us compare similarities between the two.

| DWELLING IN THE PROMISED LAND | LIVING A SPIRIT-FILLED LIFE |
| --- | --- |
| Entered by crossing the River Jordan | Entered through baptism with the Holy Spirit |
| Joshua led the people through the River Jordan. | Jesus baptises us with the Holy Spirit (John 1:33-34). |
| After crossing over, "... the LORD magnified Joshua in the sight of all Israel; and they feared him, as they feared Moses, all the days of his life." (Joshua 4:14) | After we are filled with the Holy Spirit, Jesus is magnified as we are enabled to be bold and effective witnesses to Him. Peter demonstrated this on the day of Pentecost (Acts 2:22-24). |
| Israel's diet was changed from manna (their wilderness provision) to the fruit of the land of Canaan (Joshua 5:12). | Our diet is changed from knowing Jesus only as the Saviour who died for our sins, to apprehending Him in the power of His resurrection, the spiritual realm becoming a living reality in our experience (Ephesians 1:15-23). |
| Walled cities and enemies were in the land. These were to be overcome only by total reliance on and obedience to the LORD (Joshua 5:13 – 6:27). | After being filled with the Holy Spirit, we soon perceive the reality of the powers of darkness arrayed against us. Nevertheless, clothed in *"the whole armour of God"*, we will be victorious over them (Ephesians 6:10-20). |
| A significant proportion of Israel did not want to cross the Jordan and chose an inheritance outside of Canaan. This discouraged those of God's people who desired to obey Him and inherit the Promised Land (Numbers 32:1-42). | Many Christians, and indeed whole denominations, reject the need to be baptised with the Holy Spirit, satisfying themselves with an inheritance far short of God's intentions for His Church. This discourages many from even asking God to fulfil this precious promise to them. |

One final thought before moving on to look at some other interesting parallels: is it without significance that God chose the River Jordan as the place to anoint His Son with the Holy Spirit?

Let us reiterate that we are not seeking to prove the doctrine of baptism with the Holy Spirit from typology in the Old Testament. The New Testament clearly teaches the doctrine when allowed to speak for itself. What we are doing is to identify the many parallels in the Old Testament which the thoughtful reader will realise cannot be coincidence.

## A TASTE OF HONEY

A number of years ago, I experienced a period when the subject of 'honey' recurred with such unusual regularity that I realised the Lord was drawing my attention to it. I set about looking up every scriptural reference that mentioned honey. It was a very blessed exercise and many valuable insights were obtained. By far the most striking reference was the following episode in the life of King Saul.

*(1 Samuel 14:24)  And the men of Israel were distressed that day: for Saul had adjured the people, saying, Cursed be the man that eateth any food until evening, that I may be avenged on mine enemies. So none of the people tasted any food.*
*(1 Samuel 14:25)  And all they of the land came to a wood; and there was honey upon the ground.*
*(1 Samuel 14:26)  And when the people were come into the wood, behold, the honey dropped; but no man put his hand to his mouth: for the people feared the oath.*
*(1 Samuel 14:27)  But Jonathan heard not when his father*

*charged the people with the oath: wherefore he put forth the end of the rod that was in his hand, and dipped it in an honeycomb, and put his hand to his mouth; and his eyes were enlightened.*

*(1 Samuel 14:28) Then answered one of the people, and said, Thy father straitly charged the people with an oath, saying, Cursed be the man that eateth any food this day. And the people were faint.*

*(1 Samuel 14:29) Then said Jonathan, My father hath troubled the land: see, I pray you, how mine eyes have been enlightened, because I tasted a little of this honey.*

*(1 Samuel 14:30) How much more, if haply the people had eaten freely to day of the spoil of their enemies which they found? for had there not been now a much greater slaughter among the Philistines?*

As I read and reread this account, I prayed for an understanding of what lesson could be drawn from it for the Church in Britain. What follows is the application that I believe the Lord put on my heart.

The context of this narrative is Israel's on-going conflict with the Philistines. King Saul imposed a foolish restriction on his army who were weak, faint and in great need of sustenance. Retiring to some woods, they found themselves surrounded by honey. The honey was God's provision for His people to give them the needed strength to fight with and prevail against the Philistines. However, under Saul's leadership, they were forbidden to partake of it.

The Philistines can be seen as a graphic illustration of the powers of darkness that continuously war against the Church. Could the honey be representative of God's provision for us, namely the baptism with the Holy Spirit? King Saul would then represent the many in Church leadership today who have, for various reasons, suppressed this vital truth for far too long. Just as the honey lay within easy reach for Saul's army, so the truth of the baptism with the Holy Spirit lies within easy reach for us, if we will but search the Scriptures.

There is yet more to glean from chapter 14 of 1 Samuel before moving on. If you will read from the beginning of the chapter, you will note the amazing victory over the Philistines that God granted Jonathan, Saul's son. This was achieved without the rest of the army by a man whose faith and wisdom far exceeded his father's. Being about the Lord's true work meant Jonathan was absent from the ranks when Saul issued his foolish prohibition. When Jonathan returned to the rest of the army in the woods, he too was famished and weak. He therefore did the sensible thing and ate some of the honey. It is interesting to note that those who saw him do it could see that it made an immediate difference to his appearance (verse 27). Is there not a similarity here with the very noticeable effects that were observed when various people were filled with the Holy Spirit in the Book of Acts?

I heartily recommend a character study of King Saul and of David, who was later to replace him as king. God's rebellious people had become disenchanted with His rule over them and desired to emulate the surrounding nations by having a king over them. Despite being warned what this king would be like, they were determined to have their own way (1 Samuel 8:11-20). God gave them Saul. Despite having some good qualities, his incomplete obedience to the Word of God was his downfall. David, on the other hand, was a man after God's own heart (Acts 13:22). It is interesting to note that once David appeared on the scene, it was not long before Saul became envious of him and began to seek his harm. Very soon there was that oft repeated scriptural paradox as Saul reigned in a palace whilst God's man, David, was on the run, living in obscurity and dwelling in caves. Although he was not perfect, is it not a wonderful endorsement of David's character that God should make him the most prominent ancestor of the Lord Jesus Christ?

Do you not think it strange that we can read these accounts, recognising the sin and folly, and yet be blind to identical sin and folly in our own churches? Has it not too often suited us to sit under Saul-like leaders who fail to preach the whole counsel of God? Perhaps this is because we don't like to be challenged and would rather remain *"at ease in Zion"*. Should we not be praying that God would open the eyes of our Sauls, pour out His Spirit upon them and turn them into Davids?

## THE BLOCKED WELLS

At the beginning of chapter 1, we mentioned a series of sermons on revival, preached by Dr Martyn Lloyd Jones in 1959. His text for a number of these was the Genesis account of Isaac's well digging.

*(Genesis 26:17)  And Isaac departed thence, and pitched his tent in the valley of Gerar, and dwelt there.*
*(Genesis 26:18)  And Isaac digged again the wells of water, which they had digged in the days of Abraham his father; for the Philistines had stopped them after the death of Abraham: and he called their names after the names by which his father had called them.*

The Doctor, as he was affectionately known, brought out some superb spiritual truths regarding the Western Church's much-needed revival from this Old Testament passage. Some of the following thoughts are borrowed from his insights, whereas others came after meditating further upon the passage.

The context of this account is particularly interesting. By reading from the beginning of the chapter, you will notice that famine in the land was the reason that Isaac headed south towards Egypt. We have already seen that Egypt is a 'type' of the world. Water is often used in Scripture as symbolic of the Holy Spirit.

*(John 7:37)* *In the last day, that great day of the feast, Jesus stood and cried, saying, If any man thirst, let him come unto me, and* **drink.**

*(John 7:38)* *He that believeth on me, as the scripture hath said, out of his belly shall flow rivers of* **living water.**

*(John 7:39)* **(But this spake he of the Spirit,** *which they that believe on him should receive: for the Holy Ghost was not yet given; because that Jesus was not yet glorified.)*

The Church, when conscious of a loss of spiritual power, has often reacted in the same way that Isaac did. Instead of humbling ourselves and confessing our need to God we 'head for Egypt'. Whereas in times past the Holy Spirit directed the meetings of the saints with a heavenly freshness and spontaneity, today this has been largely replaced with carefully choreographed gatherings that rely heavily upon programmes, music and even entertainment. Whilst these things might give the illusion that 'things are happening' in our midst, the reality is that we have been suffering a spiritual drought for very many years now. Even in gatherings that are largely free of these things, there can be a dryness and predictability about the meetings. The painful result of all this is clear. A famished and dehydrated Church is having almost no impact at all in our country, which is presently in spiritual and moral 'free-fall'. Isaac's urgent need for water mirrors our critical need for an outpouring of the Holy Spirit upon individual believers and the Church as a whole.

Let us not shrink from realising that God in His sovereignty sent the famine into Isaac's circumstances. Trying occurrences are often used by God to train His people in the walk of faith. However, there is another sort of drought and famine that is arguably far more serious than a literal and physical one.

*Behold, the days come, saith the Lord GOD, that I will send a famine in the land, not a famine of bread, nor a thirst for water, but of hearing the words of the LORD:* (Amos 8:11)

God can just as easily send a famine of hearing His Word as a literal famine. If His people, despite repeated admonitions, remain unfruitful under the faithful preaching of the Word and reject any of its precepts, He will act in discipline. We know from the letters to the seven churches in the book of Revelation that God will remove their testimony to Himself when a local church fails to repent after receiving correction from His Word.

*Remember therefore from whence thou art fallen, and **repent**, and do the first works; or else I will come unto thee quickly, **and will remove thy candlestick** (lampstand) out of his place, **except thou repent**.* (Revelation 2:5)

Many Western churches have either been closed or given over to the futility of false doctrine, which has rendered them useless as regards true testimony to God. Perhaps a reader is thinking to themself that their assembly is not like that, as it continues to preach faithfully from the Bible. Whilst we rejoice if that is true, is there yet something missing? If the Word constitutes food for the believer, what would be the equivalent of water? We can survive for a little while without food, but without water our life would very soon expire. Likewise, today's so-called 'Bible-believing' churches might be very orthodox in their Gospel preaching but, if they deny their need of an enduing with power from on high, their testimony is feeble indeed without the mighty energy of the Holy Spirit.

Of course, God is sovereign in the giving or withholding of rain, as happened in Elijah's day. That drought was a judgement upon Israel's sin under the wicked King Ahab. More than a century later, the prophet Amos declared God's mind to Israel.

*(Amos 4:7)  And also **I have withholden the rain from you,** when there were yet three months to the harvest: and I caused it to rain upon one city, and caused it not to rain upon another city: one piece was rained upon, and the piece whereupon it rained not withered.*

*(Amos 4:8)  So two or three cities wandered unto one city, to drink water; but they were not satisfied: **yet have ye not returned unto me, saith the LORD.***

I am convinced that the corrective intention in such portions of God's Word is lost on many in the modern Church. There is often a belief that repentance is only for unbelievers who are outside the Church. Let us remember that God's words through Amos were addressed to Israel, the people of God, and not to the pagan nations surrounding them. Likewise, the words of our Lord Jesus Christ in passages like Revelation 2:5 are addressed to the Church and not the unbelieving world outside. The Church badly needs those with the gift of prophecy, through whom God can send a word, in real-time, that directly addresses our own fellowship's situation. It might be a passage of Scripture that the elders would never have thought of applying to their own assembly, but which God *is* applying to it. It might be delivered in the believer's own words. The duty of the elders is then to weigh the prophecy in the light of the Scriptures, not despise it or, worse still, declare that such gifts are 'not for today'.

*(1 Thessalonians 5:19) Quench not the Spirit.*
*(1 Thessalonians 5:20) Despise not prophesyings.*
*(1 Thessalonians 5:21) Prove all things; hold fast that which is good.*

It is interesting to note in the Amos passage, that God caused it to rain in one city but not in another. Just as God is able to withhold or give the rain in a particular location, so He is also able to withhold or grant the outpouring of the Holy Spirit upon the Church in any geographical area. What is His purpose in doing this? Is it not designed to get His people's attention? It is impossible to ignore a literal drought for very long because water is so fundamental to life itself. It was the prophet's calling to declare to God's people that their sin had shut up the heavens. God then rebukes His people for their insensitivity to His chastening.

In today's Church, God is pouring out the Holy Spirit in some parts of the world such as China, but not in countries like Britain. One of the reasons for this is that Britain has had the blessing of the Gospel for centuries but, tragically, much of the professing church has fallen for various false teachings and many have descended into outright apostasy. Clearly God can never sanction such a 'church' with an outpouring of His Spirit. The Holy Spirit is also the Spirit of Truth and therefore will not grant His patronage to falsehood of any kind. This explains why there has never been a genuine revival in the Roman Catholic Church or indeed in any of the other cults such as the Jehovah's Witnesses.

However, this does not explain why there is such a drought in the great majority of Britain's Bible-believing fellowships. How has this come about? Yesteryear witnessed some mighty moves of God by His Spirit in this country, producing revivals in the 18th century during the time of Whitefield and the Wesleys, 1859 in Wales and Northern Ireland and, more recently, between 1949 and 1953 in the Hebrides. Nevertheless, the history of revivals clearly demonstrates that the dramatically improved condition of the Church is not permanent. It is as if God gradually reduces the outpouring, but the church, instead of properly understanding the source of her power, tries to keep things going in her own strength. Inevitably, this will not work and the number of conversions seen drops off to almost nil. The temptation then comes to adopt programmes, courses and an endless round of activities in an attempt to substitute for lost spiritual power. This seems to be much more palatable to many than humbly confessing our need to God and waiting upon Him in prayer for another outpouring of His Holy Spirit.

Returning to Isaac now and his urgent need for water, let us see what spiritual lessons can be learned from his actions.

Firstly, there is no substitute for water and so obtaining it was Isaac's top priority. There is no substitute for the Holy Spirit; is being filled with the Holy Spirit our top priority? Isaac did not waste time digging new wells, but instead went straight for the ones his father Abraham before him had dug. Do we go back to the promise of our Father in His Word, or are we seeking spiritual strength in some other way? It is very interesting to notice that the Philistines had maliciously blocked the wells that Abraham had dug by filling them with earth.

*For all the wells which his father's servants had dug in the days of Abraham his father, the Philistines had stopped them and filled them with earth. (Genesis 26:15)*

Very often when a believer determines to seek God concerning His promise of the Holy Spirit's filling, he or she will soon find that the modern 'Philistines' have been at work. They have sought to render the promise ineffective by hurling the 'earth' of false teaching into the 'well' of God's Word. Isaac set about clearing the earth from the wells and was rewarded for his efforts with the much sought-after water. We too can clear the false teaching, unbelief and discouragement from our 'wells' by diligently searching the relevant Scriptures and praying for a correct understanding of them. To our joy, we will find that the promise of the Father is made good to us.

Before moving on, is there not another lesson for us in noting that, referring to the wells, Isaac *"called their names after the names by which his father had called them" (Genesis 26:18)*? He did not make up new names for the wells but called them by their original names. Today, one sometimes hears the baptism with the Holy Spirit being referred to as 'the second blessing'. You might ask what the problem with that is. For one thing, it is far more vague and indistinct and, unless clearly defined by the context of a conversation, could leave someone confused as to precisely what was being spoken about. Doubtless, to be baptised with the Holy Spirit is a blessing, but that is not its primary purpose. I've never heard *salvation* being referred to as 'the first blessing', although one could hardly conceive of a greater blessing! The term 'salvation' has a distinct meaning, as does the phrase 'baptism with the Holy Spirit'. Many readers will be aware that this teaching is controversial, but is that really surprising when we remember that the Devil opposes every vital Christian doctrine? By being careless with our terms, we help opponents of this truth to hide behind indistinct terminology. However, most importantly of all, our Lord Jesus Christ referred to the enduing with power from on high as being, *"…baptized with the Holy Spirit…" (Acts 1:5)*. Therefore we would surely be wise to do the same.

## WHERE ARE THE SMITHS?

*(1 Samuel 13:19)* **Now there was no smith** (blacksmith) *found throughout all the land of Israel: for the Philistines said, Lest the Hebrews make them swords or spears:*

*(1 Samuel 13:20) But all the Israelites went down to the Philistines, to sharpen every man his share, and his coulter, and his axe, and his mattock.*

*(1 Samuel 13:21) Yet they had a file for the mattocks, and for the coulters, and for the forks, and for the axes, and to sharpen the goads.*

*(1 Samuel 13:22)* **So it came to pass in the day of battle, that there was neither sword nor spear found in the hand of any of the people** *that were with Saul and Jonathan: but with Saul and with Jonathan his son was there found.*

*(1 Samuel 13:23) And the garrison of the Philistines went out to the passage of Michmash.*

In this very interesting passage we find Israel in a state of weakness and subjection to the Philistines. Just as in Isaac's time, when the Philistines had blocked the wells, so now they had removed all of the blacksmiths from the land. This meant that none of Israel's soldiers had swords and so were very little threat to the Philistines. The Israelites were only allowed to have agricultural implements and even had to go to the Philistines to get these sharpened. What a picture of an impoverished Western church going to the world to borrow its methods for church growth. It is not surprising to find this state of affairs existing under Saul's leadership. Just as in the incident with the forbidden honey, we find Israel unable to stand against its enemies due to a lack of essential equipping. Again, it is not difficult to see the parallel between this situation and a Church trying to function without the power of the Holy Spirit that God has promised.

## A WISE DAUGHTER'S REQUEST

*(Joshua 15:16) And Caleb said, He that smiteth Kirjathsepher, and taketh it, to him will I give Achsah my daughter to wife.*
*(Joshua 15:17) And Othniel the son of Kenaz, the brother of Caleb, took it: and he gave him Achsah his daughter to wife.*
*(Joshua 15:18) And it came to pass, as she came unto him, that she moved him to ask of her father a field: and she lighted off her ass; and Caleb said unto her, What wouldest thou?*
*(Joshua 15:19) Who answered, Give me a blessing; for thou hast given me a south land; give me also springs of water. And he gave her the upper springs, and the nether springs.*

In this lovely passage we are introduced to Achsah, the daughter of Caleb. It is very significant that Caleb had been one of the two spies who gave a faithful report of the land all those years previously (see Numbers 13:30). He had obviously trained Achsah well in the things of God and she grew into a wise young woman. When she approached her father, she was already the possessor of an inheritance from him. Yet, realising that this "south land" was arid and, on its own, not conducive to an abundantly fruitful future, she asked him for an additional inheritance of springs of water. Observe how, without hesitation, her father granted her not only springs of water, but "upper springs" and "nether (or lower) springs". This is a delightful outworking of the words of the Lord Jesus Christ:

*If ye then, being evil, know how to give good gifts unto your children: how much more shall your heavenly Father give the Holy Spirit to them that ask him?* (Luke 11:13)

We see here a human father giving good gifts to his daughter, just as our Lord intimated. Can you see in this a further illustration of the principle in which a believer, who has already inherited salvation, draws near to his or her heavenly Father and asks to be baptised with the Holy Spirit? The words of our Lord Jesus encourage us to realise "how much more" our heavenly Father is ready to bestow this much-needed gift.

## OTHER EXAMPLES

There are other examples illustrating the same pattern that we have seen so far. If one carefully reads Numbers 21:5-24, an instructive sequence emerges:

| REFERENCE | OCCURRENCE | CHRISTIAN PARALLEL |
| --- | --- | --- |
| Numbers 21:8-9 | Bronze serpent made and lifted up. Those who had been bitten by snakes lived if they looked upon the bronze serpent. | Salvation. Those who recognise themselves to be sinners are saved when they look to the Lord Jesus Christ and his blood shed for them upon the Cross. |
| Numbers 21:10-13 | Journeying through the wilderness. | The Christian walk prior to being baptised with the Holy Spirit. |
| Numbers 21:16-18 | Arrived at the well, spoken of by the LORD. In faith, they sang in expectancy of water before it was actually obtained. The princes dug using only their staves. Possibly the well was obscured only by a shallow layer of brushwood, sand and rubble. Water obtained. | Hearing about the promised baptism with the Holy Spirit. The brushwood of misunderstanding, the sand of unbelief and the rubble of wrong teaching are removed by able Christian leaders using only the staves of sound teaching, prayer and encouragement. Baptism with the Holy Spirit obtained. |
| Numbers 21:19-24 | Refreshed, Israel marched on with renewed strength. Opposition soon encountered in the form of the Amorites. Israel victorious over them and possessed their land. | Filled with joy and strength, the Christian now experiences the *reality* of walking in the Spirit. Spiritual opposition soon comes, but God enables the Spirit-filled believer to overcome. |

## CONCLUSION

The distinction between initial conversion and subsequent baptism with the Holy Spirit is clearly established in the New Testament. In the foregoing Old Testament examples, we have been seeking to show that there are many interesting and instructive illustrations that foreshadow the New Testament pattern. Doubtless, the reader will be able to find other similar examples.

CHAPTER 6

# HOW TRUTH IS SUPPRESSED

Before we look into different ways in which truth is suppressed, it would be profitable to note the prominence that God gives in His Word to preachers and teachers speaking *all* of His words rather than just *most* of them. If the reader has the facility, either on a computer or electronic concordance, try a word search using the phrase, 'all words'. You will find a very large number of instances in which God is careful to command His spokesmen to speak *all* of His words to the people. The following verses are just a small sample of these, with some others on the same theme.

*Thus saith the LORD; Stand in the court of the LORD'S house, and speak unto all the cities of Judah, which come to worship in the LORD'S house,* **all the words** *that I command thee to speak unto them;* **diminish not a word***: (Jeremiah 26:2)*

*Moreover he said unto me, Son of man,* **all my words** *that I shall speak unto thee receive in thine heart, and hear with thine ears. (Ezekiel 3:10)*

*Teaching them to observe* **all things whatsoever I have commanded you***: and, lo, I am with you alway, even unto the end of the world. Amen. (Matthew 28:20)*

*Then he said unto them, O fools, and slow of heart to believe* **all that the prophets have spoken***:* *(Luke 24:25)*

*Go, stand and speak in the temple to the people* **all the words** *of this life. (Acts 5:20)*

*For I have not shunned to declare unto you* **all the counsel of God***. (Acts 20:27)*

We can see from these verses that the word *'all'* is a very small word with a very large meaning. If we teach or preach, we ignore this vital principle at our peril!

## CORRECTING ERROR WITH ERROR

Many years ago I read a particular commentary whilst studying a controversial Bible doctrine. A very pithy observation was made concerning a tendency seen throughout Church history. Although being applied to one particular doctrine, the principle applies to any other key teaching. It noted that, just as in the case of the Lord Jesus Christ, the truth is often 'crucified' between a left-hand and a right-hand thief. The point being made was that, if the Church gradually veers off into a particular doctrinal error (let's call it 'left-hand error'), those who recognise the problem have a tendency to overreact and steer the Church into an equal and opposite error ('right-hand error') to compensate. No doubt the Devil does not mind which error the Church is in, as long as it *is* error. A similar analogy would be that of the pendulum swinging first to one extreme and then to the other. The right way to correct doctrinal error is by the prayerful and accurate use of the Word of God, as directed by the Holy

Spirit. The Holy Spirit always leads us back to the truth as it is in the Word, whereas the Devil drives men from one error into another.

*Howbeit when he, the Spirit of truth, is come, **he will guide you into all truth**: for he shall not speak of himself; but whatsoever he shall hear, that shall he speak: and he will shew you things to come.* (John 16:13)

Perhaps the reader has experienced something akin to the foregoing in their own church life. This author has had to face it several times. The following example serves to illustrate the problem.

An otherwise able speaker visited our assembly to conduct the evening ministry. It soon became clear that the purpose of his message was to turn people away from the teaching that there was such a thing as the baptism with the Holy Spirit to be sought after by today's believers. He also concluded that we should not be seeking the gifts of the Holy Spirit. What were the grounds upon which he based his assertions? He spent most of his message giving a long list of notorious false teachers and charlatans along with their antics supposedly performed by the power of the Holy Spirit. He implied that this is how one would end up if one persisted in seeking spiritual gifts. The more astute reader will realise that this is not the way to arrive at the truth. It is what is known as a 'straw man' argument. Using this tactic, the speaker selects a well-known charlatan (the 'straw man') and claims that he is a typical example of those who teach the baptism with the Holy Spirit. The speaker then 'knocks down' the 'straw man', which is hardly difficult to do. He then implies to his hearers that he has thus disproved the doctrine of the baptism with the Holy Spirit. I need hardly add that this sort of thing has no place in serious Bible exposition. The humiliating truth is that we can easily become so afraid of the false that we end up rejecting the true. Is the solution to drink-driving a ban on *all* drivers from our roads?

Revealingly, on one memorable occasion a dear older brother, who might be described as a Brethren grandee, confided in me that he had never heard an *honest* exposition of Scripture proving that the gifts of the Holy Spirit had ceased!

Some years ago I read a very interesting testimony by a man who had been in a Brethren assembly for many years. It was an online article that I have been unable to find again in recent searches. Nevertheless, I can recall the details that are pertinent to our subject. Whether he was told of the baptism with the Holy Spirit by someone, or whether he discovered it for himself whilst reading the Scriptures, I cannot remember. However, the important thing is that, despite the cessationist teaching surrounding him, he received the baptism with the Holy Spirit. He described the joy and radical transformation it made to his Christian life, which those readers who have also received this precious gift will readily identify with. He then began to try and figure out what it was in Brethren teaching that had so effectively suppressed teaching on this promise of God and kept him in the dark for so long. Unfortunately he came to the conclusion that 'dispensational' doctrine was to blame, so he left the Brethren and joined a reformed church, embracing its amillennial teaching. Whilst we rejoice at this brother's filling with the Holy Spirit, we lament that he had effectively exchanged one error for another (i.e. amillennialism).

There is no incompatibility between teaching the baptism with the Holy Spirit and a dispensational understanding of the Bible. The problem comes when dispensationalism is pushed beyond what is revealed in the Scriptures. Cessationists do this by effectively inventing an extra 'mini' dispensation between Pentecost and, typically, the time when the Canon of Scripture was completed. They allow that the Church was equipped with supernatural spiritual gifts in this narrow timeframe. However, they claim that God caused them to cease after that, hence the name cessationism. This teaching cannot be substantiated from the Scriptures and is a major reason for bringing the perfectly valid system of dispensational interpretation into disrepute.

## THE DANGERS OF GOOD MINISTRY

Are you wondering whether you read that subtitle correctly? Imagine for a moment the meals that we eat each day. Hopefully, we have a well-balanced diet with all the essential nutrients present, but what would happen if one vital ingredient was constantly missing? Even though all the rest of the ingredients were very good and there was no poison present, we would soon start to exhibit symptoms of deteriorating health. We would become weak and sickly and perhaps eventually die. Now picture this as an analogy of good weekly ministry of the Word, but with one important truth constantly missing. Perhaps the majority of the hearers do not realise there is something missing because they have never heard of it. The weak condition of their church is considered normal because they have never known anything else.

In his "Morning by Morning" devotional for 4th August, C H Spurgeon said the following:

*"How can we hope for a thing if we do not know of its existence? Hope may be the telescope, but until we receive instruction, our ignorance stands in front of the glass, and we can see nothing whatever; knowledge removes the interposing object, and when we look through the bright optic glass we discern the glory to be revealed, and anticipate it with joyous confidence."*

In my experience, Brethren assemblies are blessed with much good ministry. However, the experience of Spirit-filled believers who occasionally visit their meetings is, invariably, a stifling sense that 'something is missing'. How has this state of affairs been perpetuated?

Visiting speakers are invariably from other Brethren assemblies and can usually be relied upon to toe the party line. If they did not, their time on the speaking circuit would soon be curtailed. Add to this that the majority of assembly members only ever read or listen to Brethren material. Whilst this is very effective at keeping things like the 'Toronto Blessing' and a host of modern false prophets from their doors, there is a real downside. Highly gifted preachers and teachers from 'outside', who are able to skilfully teach on matters such as the baptism with the Holy Spirit, are also kept out. This creates a situation where long-standing error is 'locked in' and continues virtually unchallenged. As alluded to earlier in the chapter, if it is perceived that some within an assembly might be discussing the whole matter of being baptised with the Holy Spirit, it is not usually long before a visiting speaker comes with a mandate to pour cold water on it. Great lengths are gone to in order to present cessationist doctrine as scriptural and therefore respectable. Thus a precious truth is suppressed.

## STUDY BIBLES AND COMMENTARIES

Study Bibles and commentaries can be a great help in studying the Scriptures, but they can also be misleading. The danger comes when readers regard the study notes as being inspired in the same way that the Scriptures themselves are. The MacArthur Study Bible is one of the most popular available today and is, by all accounts, a high quality piece of work. Even so, if it was read uncritically, it would lead the reader into cessationist beliefs. This author owns an excellent study Bible from yesteryear that is a great help in many respects. However, it too would lead readers into cessationist beliefs if its comments were regarded as authoritative. Should we then throw out such study Bibles and commentaries? Of course not! The answer lies in a mature realisation that the authors of reputable study Bibles and commentaries are passing on, in all sincerity, their best understanding of pertinent passages of scripture at the time of writing. Therefore we can avoid suppressing an important truth by using study Bibles and commentaries wisely.

## HYBRID CESSATIONISM?

More recently, I have come across an unusual doctrinal position that appears to mix an element of cessationism with an acceptance that the gifts of the Holy Spirit are for today. The stance that I am about to describe is taken by a fellowship known to the author, although I hasten to add that most other fellowships linked to the same group would not subscribe to it.

They teach that all believers are *automatically* baptised with the Holy Spirit at the point of their conversion. This is basically the same as cessationists teach and, as I hope that we have already demonstrated, cannot be squared with Scripture. This is where the similarity with cessationist teaching ends. They then teach that all believers have *already* been given certain gifts of the Holy Spirit and simply need to discover what these are. At first, this might sound plausible. However, in Scripture, Christians *never* manifested supernatural spiritual gifts until *after* they had been baptised with the Holy Spirit.

Consistent with their doctrine, they encourage believers to 'go on being filled with the Holy Spirit'. Again, this sounds plausible based on the teaching of Ephesians 5:18. The problem with this is that you cannot 'go on being filled' if you have never *first* been filled. There must be a *first* time. As we saw in chapter 4, the way to be filled with the Holy Spirit is to go in faith to our heavenly Father and Ask, Seek, Knock. Once we have been filled with the Holy Spirit, then, and only then, can we see to it that we go on being filled by asking God every day in prayer.

What has been the practical outworking of this teaching in this church? Despite members being told that they already have these gifts, there has been no manifestation of them over the years. This is a bit like the 'Emperor's New Clothes' scenario and would legitimately attract Dr Martyn Lloyd Jones' question we quoted in chapter 1:

*"I know that all of you would want to say to my question about the Holy Spirit, 'Well, we got it all at conversion; there's*

*no need for any more experience.' "Well," said Martyn Lloyd-Jones, "I have only one other question to ask you. If you got it all at conversion, where in God's name is it?"*

Although the position described is a little different to classic cessationism, it actually produces precisely the same result; that is to say a fellowship in which many have never been baptised with the Holy Spirit and therefore possess none of His spiritual gifts. When the 'line by line' teaching ministry of this church reached 1 Corinthians 14, necessitating teaching on the spiritual gifts and their correct use, the absence of any evidence of spiritual gifts amongst the membership was effectively glossed over. Compelled to explain the contrast between themselves and a church where the gifts are in operation, it was rationalised as being merely a difference in style of meeting. I would contend that the reality is not a difference in *style* but a difference in *substance*. It seems the height of irony that people should be instructed in the correct use of the spiritual gifts and warned about their abuse, when many do not possess any to either use or abuse. Even those who have been baptised with the Holy Spirit and exercised gifts in the past, in reality do not feel free to use them in the meetings.

Many readers will no doubt wonder how it is possible to arrive at such a 'hybrid' doctrinal position. On discussing it with their pastor I was told that we must not take our doctrine from 'narrative' portions of Scripture, but must only take it from the epistles. He went on to say that you could prove any doctrine that you liked from the 'narrative' sections, by which he meant the Gospels and the Book of Acts. Many readers will no doubt already have thought of the following verse from one of the epistles:

***All scripture*** *is given by inspiration of God, and is **profitable** **for doctrine**, for reproof, **for correction**, for instruction in righteousness: (2 Timothy 3:16)*

In the light of this verse, the only way one can exclude the Gospels and Acts from being *"profitable for doctrine"* is to declare that they are not Scripture. Clearly this is not a position many Bible teachers would want to adopt.

After a recent ministry meeting, I had the opportunity of discussing this strange, 'hybrid' doctrinal position with a well-known and respected Bible expositor. Apart from affirming the need for believers to be baptised with the Holy Spirit, he made reference to the following verses in an epistle:

*(1 Corinthians 10:1)  Moreover, brethren, I would not that ye should be ignorant, how that all our fathers were **under the cloud**, and all passed through the sea;*
*(1 Corinthians 10:2)  And were all baptized unto*(into) *Moses **in the cloud** and in the sea;*

In the first thirteen verses of 1 Corinthians chapter 10, the apostle Paul is using the example of Israel's history to teach spiritual lessons, just as we did in chapter 5. Notice that in verse 2, there are effectively three baptisms referred to. These are, (i) into Moses, (ii) in the cloud and (iii) in the sea. The baptism "into Moses" was an acknowledgement by the people that Moses was God's appointed leader and of their identification with him; the parallel for us is our baptism into the body of Christ at the point of conversion. The cloud was a visible manifestation of God's presence to guide and protect His people; the parallel for us is the baptism with the Holy Spirit that will result in a manifestation of God's Spirit for the edification of the Church:

*But the manifestation of the Spirit is given to every man to profit withal.  (1 Corinthians 12:7)*

The baptism in the sea separated Israel from Egypt; the parallel for us is baptism in water, which is symbolic of our separation from the world and its sin. The order in 1 Corinthians 10:2 does not teach that baptism with the Holy Spirit must always precede baptism in water. It is clear from the Book of Acts that the order was not always the same; in Acts chapter 8 the Samaritan believers were first baptised in water and subsequently with the Holy Spirit; in Acts chapter 10 Cornelius and his household were first baptised with the Holy Spirit and afterwards in water.

## SHRINKING BACK

In many Bible believing fellowships that deny the baptism with the Holy Spirit, a remarkable paradox can often be found. Amongst the membership there can be discovered some who have been baptised with the Holy Spirit in the past, but who now oppose the doctrine and have ceased to use any gifts they may have been given. But for the grace of God, this author very nearly came to that position in the mid-90s. How and why does this happen?

I believe that the most common reason is a bad experience in a previous fellowship that has gone off the rails and into what we might call 'charismania'. In such circles, spiritual experiences begin to replace the objective Word of God as the measure of what is good and true. This is a recipe for disaster. The last two decades have witnessed rapidly escalating spiritual deception within the professing church.

In the 1990s we had the so-called 'Toronto Blessing', where people were overcome with uncontrollable laughter, shaking and even making bizarre animal noises etc. Some church leaders actually flew to Toronto to 'get it' and bring it back to impart to their own congregations. To attribute these sorts of things to the work of the Holy Spirit represents a catastrophic departure from Biblical discernment. The downhill slide has only accelerated since then. Whilst some churches might not have embraced all of these things, they have routinely accepted puerile 'prophecies' that would not stand up to the test of the Word, misused tongues, given spurious 'words' to individuals and literally fallen for the 'slain in the spirit' experience.

When true Christians, who love the Word of God, find themselves in such a fellowship it can be very distressing for them. The experience of most who have warned the leadership of their concerns, is that it usually falls on deaf ears. The only option remaining is to leave and try to find a church that is Biblically sound. The sense of relief in finally finding such a church is huge and, if the teaching ministry is particularly good, one can be forgiven for feeling that one has finally 'arrived'. However, with painful memories of 'charismania' still in our minds, we can all too easily adopt the mindset that our new pastor cannot be wrong in anything he teaches. We still need to be 'Bereans' no matter who is doing the preaching and teaching. Could it be that the welcome absence of 'charismania' in our new church is also accompanied by a mournful absence of the *real* work of the Holy Spirit?

In chapter 5 we looked at some remarkable events in Israel's history that have a spiritual parallel in Christian experience. In particular, we looked at crossing the River

Jordan into the Promised Land as being illustrative of the baptism with the Holy Spirit. Are there any instances that would illustrate God's people shrinking back to a place of perceived safety, motivated by fear rather than faith?

*(1 Samuel 13:5) And the Philistines gathered themselves together to fight with Israel, thirty thousand chariots, and six thousand horsemen, and people as the sand which is on the sea shore in multitude: and they came up, and pitched in Michmash, eastward from Bethaven.*
*(1 Samuel 13:6) When the men of Israel saw that they were in a strait, (**for the people were distressed**,) then the people did hide themselves in caves, and in thickets, and in rocks, and in high places, and in pits.*
*(1 Samuel 13:7)* ***And some of the Hebrews went over Jordan to the land of Gad and Gilead.*** *As for Saul, he was yet in Gilgal, and all the people followed him trembling.*

Notice how in verse 7 some of God's people fled back over the Jordan and out of the Promised Land. To act in such a way demonstrated that they had lost sight of the God of Israel entirely and were consequently driven by fear. Can you see in this a graphic illustration of how some Christians, who once knew the power of the Holy Spirit, act in the face of intimidating spiritual deceptions and counterfeits? An interesting quote from Martin Luther makes a similar point and warns against acting in such a way:

*"If I profess with the loudest voice and clearest exposition every portion of the truth of God **except precisely that little point which the world and the devil are at that moment attacking**, I am not confessing Christ, however boldly I may be professing Christ. **Where the battle rages, there the loyalty***

***of the soldier is proved***; *and to be steady on all the battlefield besides is mere flight and disgrace if he flinches at that point."*

To be sure, there is a battle raging over the whole matter of the baptism with the Holy Spirit. It is desperately opposed by Satan and, sadly, by many believers who have heeded his advice to get as far away from it as they can.

If you know that you have been baptised with the Holy Spirit and exercised a spiritual gift or gifts in the past, but have allowed yourself to be intimidated into denying the whole matter, what should you do? May I lovingly encourage you to turn back to the Lord in repentance, confessing that you have grieved and quenched His Holy Spirit? He will most certainly forgive you, fill you anew with the Holy Spirit and *"will restore to you the years that the locust hath eaten"*. Do not allow the unbelief and disobedience of others to rob you of God's riches. It might just be that God wants to use *you* to awaken the corner of His Church in which He has placed you.

## BELIEVING, BUT LINGERING

After our consideration of those who 'shrink back', we need to mention those whose position is nearly the opposite. Ironically, there are some within cessationist fellowships who know in their hearts that this aspect of their assembly's teaching is wrong but, for reasons known only to themselves, choose to do nothing about it. They are quite happy to discuss the matter, but never seem to go to the Lord in faith to obtain the promise for themselves. If we hope to make a difference, we need more than just a belief that the doctrine of the baptism with the Holy Spirit is true; we need to actually *be* baptised with the Holy Spirit. Doubtless there are some who linger in this position for a quiet life, knowing the sort of opposition that they are likely to encounter were they to make a stand for this truth. Hence the truth can be suppressed even by those who believe it, due to a failure to act upon it.

## FURTHER TRUTH-SUPRESSING FACTORS

### Homoeopathy

Over the years spent in Brethren assemblies, I had many conversations with fellow believers concerning the baptism with the Holy Spirit. Whilst some were prepared to listen to a scriptural argument, others were not. On one occasion during a pre-lunch conversation in someone's home, a much-loved and respected elder 'closed me down' as I tried to share thoughts on certain Scriptures with him. His reaction was as if he had been gripped by sudden fear and it was quite startling. I found this general reluctance to even discuss the subject curious and prayed to the Lord for an understanding of any underlying cause. Soon, without looking for it, I gradually became aware that homoeopathic medicine was widely used in Brethren circles. How is this relevant to our subject? In what follows, I am not implying that homoeopathy is the main factor behind Brethren suppression of a separate baptism with the Holy Spirit, but that it appears to be a significant one.

It is not my purpose to write a lengthy exposé of homoeopathy's origins, since this has already been done by several authors. Suffice it to say that the roots of the practice are buried deep in the occult. In the West, we seem to be particularly slow to understand the Biblical principle that the roots or origins of an issue determine its true nature. No matter how cunningly a system is disguised in innocent-looking contemporary garb, if the roots are in darkness then the true nature of the practice is also darkness.

The following verses illustrate that, just as in the natural world, the true character of a spiritual matter is determined by its roots or origin.

*For if the firstfruit be holy, the lump is also holy: and if the root be holy, so are the branches.* (Romans 11:16)

Although the context of this verse concerns the truth about Israel, the principle it teaches is universally applicable. Obviously the opposite also holds good; if the root is unholy, so are the branches. The Lord Jesus also taught this principle in the context of His warning about false prophets.

*(Matthew 7:17) Even so every good tree bringeth forth good fruit; but a corrupt tree bringeth forth evil fruit.*

*(Matthew 7:18) A good tree cannot bring forth evil fruit, neither can a corrupt tree bring forth good fruit.*

Advocates of homoeopathy would no doubt be quick to claim that its 'fruits' are good and therefore no further questions need be asked. This ignores the well-documented origins of the practice and is naive concerning Satan's subtlety in making evil look good.

*Lest Satan should get an advantage of us: for we are not ignorant of his devices.* (2 Corinthians 2:11)

*And no marvel; for Satan himself is transformed into an angel of light.* (2 Corinthians 11:14)

*Put on the whole armour of God, that ye may be able to stand against the wiles of the devil. (Ephesians 6:11)*

Again, whilst being mindful of the context of these verses, there is obviously a much wider application of these truths.

Many believers who are involved with homoeopathy would claim that there is nothing 'spiritual' about it and that it is just another form of medicine. Yet the practice defies all scientific attempts to determine *how* it works. If it works at all (which many dispute), then some other force or influence must be at work since the substances used are so dilute as to be practically non-existent. The following quote is a letter from a senior doctor to the Daily Telegraph on 24 June 2009:

*"SIR – I am glad that X's (name removed – Ed) symptoms have got better (Features, June 22). However, since she never went back to her GP, we cannot know what has happened to the ovarian cyst. It may have spontaneously regressed, or burst, or may not have been the source of her pain.*

*I have no problem with people treating minor ailments by taking sugar pills with active ingredients diluted to the point of being undetectable, as they often remit spontaneously in any event. To suggest homoeopathy, however, for the treatment of ovarian cysts should be of great concern, not least because they can be cancerous.*

*Just because X, undoubtedly an expert on tennis, subscribes to a belief system that has more in common with witchcraft than any kind of rationality, does not make it any more credible."*

I believe that this doctor is very close to the truth in his final paragraph. Being a belief system implies that a certain 'faith' is required of its adherents. This is exactly what one finds when trying to warn fellow believers who are involved with it. They frequently become defensive and are often unwilling to enter into meaningful dialogue. This is a great pity since there is almost certainly much more at stake than they realise.

What has all of this got to do with the baptism with the Holy Spirit? At the beginning of this subsection I mentioned praying to God for an understanding of what might underlie the curious blindness concerning the Holy Spirit, which seems to prevail throughout the Brethren movement. I should say here that this phenomenon is not unique to the Brethren, but that is where much of my experience lies. I believe the Lord revealed that homoeopathy was a significant contributory factor in Christians being closed to receiving the baptism with the Holy Spirit. Clearly there can be other factors involved, which we will look at later. Interestingly, many who have been baptised with the Holy Spirit seem gifted with a spontaneous discernment over issues such as homoeopathy. Without prior knowledge of a practice, they sense what appears to be an instinctive disquiet concerning it. This spiritual sensitivity is clearly given to them by the Holy Spirit.

What then is it about involvement with homoeopathy that would bring about a measure of spiritual blindness? The bottom line is that involvement (knowingly or unknowingly) in *any* form of the occult will give the Devil a foothold in one's life. The result will be a measure of demonic interference, whether perceived or not. The same holds true for a host of other 'New Age' practices that are flooding into a gullible professing church, such as yoga and mystical 'prayer' techniques. Obviously, Satan has an interest in preventing believers receiving the baptism with the Holy Spirit if he can.

In chapter 5, we saw an illustration of this principle as the Philistines kept Israel in a state of impotence by not allowing them any weapons of warfare. I believe homoeopathy is another instance of Satan's subtlety in making something evil look benign and even beneficial.

## Martial Arts

Many Christians do not realise that martial arts also have their roots in the occult. If they did, no doubt they would not allow their children to attend such classes. We are so used to assessing things by their outward appearance that, if *we* cannot *see* anything wrong with a practice, we conclude all is well. After all, martial arts are just a sport and a good way to keep fit, aren't they? If we have adopted that mind-set, we are likely to regard warnings about these sorts of things as being 'over the top'. There seems to be a considerable naivety about these issues in the Western church. Just as with homoeopathy, one cannot indulge in these things without running the risk of spiritual harm.

The late Stewart Dool of Intercessors for Britain (IFB) used to give very credible warnings concerning these things as part of his broad and challenging ministry. Before his conversion, he had been a karate champion as well as a rock musician. He spoke with clear authority on the matter, using perturbing examples from his own experience, which left the hearer in no doubt of the spiritual dangers involved. He also taught the importance of believers seeking the baptism with the Holy Spirit for effective witness and service.

## Rock Music

Just as there were many in ancient Israel craving to adopt the godless practices of surrounding pagan nations, so in the modern professing church there are many wanting to adopt a godless world's music to use in 'worship'. Much has been written and documentaries have been made concerning the origins of rock music and its suitability or otherwise for use by the Church. Again, the late Stewart Dool of IFB was able to shed a great deal of light on the matter as an ex-rock musician. Suffice it to say that the roots of rock music are indisputably in the occult. The very term, 'Christian rock music' is an oxymoron. Those who promote so-called 'Christian rock' claim that music is a neutral medium that can be used for good or evil. They assert that if scriptural words are put to rock music it becomes acceptable. Nothing could be further from the truth. The roots of rock music are unholy and therefore it has no place whatsoever in the worship of a holy God.

Why have we mentioned rock music in connection with the baptism with the Holy Spirit? Simply because if your church is given to this kind of music in its meetings, there is no point in seeking God for an outpouring of the Holy Spirit, since He is just that, HOLY. Another spirit might well feel at home in such meetings, but not the Holy Spirit. Likewise, if you as an individual believer are listening privately to rock music, be it 'Christian' or secular, it will have a corrosive effect on your spiritual life. One of the 20th century's greatest preachers, A W Tozer, warned that, *"If you love and listen to the wrong kind of music, your inner life will wither and die"*.

## Personal Factors

One cannot help but notice that there are a significant number of professing Christians who simply do not *want* this teaching about the baptism with the Holy Spirit to be true. They will ignore or gloss over relevant scriptures and avoid any conversation about the issue if they possibly can. Clearly this attitude and conduct is at variance with the very scriptures that many of them claim to believe. They are neither being good Bereans nor submitting themselves to the whole counsel of God. Thus they suppress this precious truth to themselves, but also have a spiritually stifling effect upon any fellowship of which they are a part.

Over many years of observation, I believe that the following are the main reasons why a lot of Christians act in this way:

## Wrong Teaching

This is probably the most obvious factor. When one has imbibed erroneous teaching for many years, it becomes deeply ingrained in one's understanding and is not easily undone. The whole purpose of this book is to try to help repair the damage. A condition that we should all guard against, particularly if we are in leadership, is that of becoming unteachable. One of the most lovely examples in the Scriptures of a very gifted and yet teachable man is surely that of Apollos (Acts 18:24-28). Although he is described as being *"mighty in the scriptures"* he was quite prepared to be taken aside by a couple of tent makers (one of them a woman) and have the way of God explained more thoroughly. As a result, the Lord greatly prospered his subsequent ministry. If only more in Church leadership had the humility of Apollos!

## Pride

Pride is a root sin that we all have to do battle with. If we give place to it, it will lead to a whole host of other sins. The sin of being unteachable, which we have just mentioned, has its roots in pride. This can be particularly difficult for a leader who has taught something publicly, perhaps over many years, but comes to realise that it is an error. Great grace is required to publicly admit to the error, but then great grace is available. I remember praising God after reading the account of a Christian leader who did just that. Marcus Luedi, in chapter 25 of his book "Room 105", described how he had accepted the false teaching ("guided visualisation") of Dr Paul Yonggi Cho in his book, "The Fourth Dimension", on the subject of healing. Luedi passed on this teaching to his own family and congregation as well as to many others where he spoke. Tragically, his wife was dying of cancer but, having imbibed and practised Yonggi Cho's teaching, he was utterly convinced that God was going to heal her. In spiritual crisis after her death, he cried to the Lord in prayer. God answered that prayer and in providence brought an elderly pastor across his path. Luedi recounted to the pastor all that had happened. The pastor then selected a book from his shelves that he felt would help Luedi in his perplexity. That book was the late Dave Hunt's "The Seduction of Christianity". As he read, God opened his eyes to the sheer scale of false teachings and practices that had been infiltrating the Church. Amongst these was what he had been teaching about healing. Having been convinced of his error, to his great credit, he set about visiting as many of the congregations that he had spoken to as was practically possible. He explained to them the reason why what he had previously taught them was wrong and instructed them in true Biblical doctrine. May God be praised for this man's humility and conscientious concern for the spiritual well-being of the Church.

> *A man's pride shall bring him low: but honour shall uphold the humble in spirit.  (Proverbs 29:23)*

## Unbelief

It would be hard to overstate the mischief suffered by individual believers and the wider Church as a result of unbelief. Salvation comes through faith in the Lord Jesus Christ, but believers often forget that the promises of God to them must also come through faith. The 'promise of the Father', the baptism with the Holy Spirit is no exception to this. Unbelief can be overcome by prayer and diligently studying the promise in God's Word, considering just who it is that has made the promise: God, who cannot lie. We are told that Israel could not enter the Promised Land because of unbelief (Hebrews 3:19). In the same way, unbelief in the promised baptism with the Holy Spirit will prevent us from receiving it. Sometimes, sadly, the unbelief that one observes appears to be wilful and stubborn, reflecting an individual's personal prejudice against and distaste for the things of the Holy Spirit. In such cases genuine repentance is needed. Would it not be so much better to emulate Abraham's faith?

> *He staggered not at the promise of God through unbelief; but was strong in faith, giving glory to God;  (Romans 4:20)*

## Fear

Fear can take different forms. No doubt there are some who have a fear over what they might get if they ask God for the Holy Spirit. It is for precisely this reason that the Lord Jesus Christ said the following in His teaching on prayer in Luke chapter 11:

*(Luke 11:11)  If a son shall ask bread of any of you that is a father, will he give him a stone? or if he ask a fish, will he for a fish give him a serpent?*

*(Luke 11:12)  Or if he shall ask an egg, will he offer him a scorpion?*

*(Luke 11:13)  If ye then, being evil, know how to give good gifts unto your children: how much more shall your heavenly Father give the Holy Spirit to them that ask him?*

These gracious words from the lips of our Saviour should be more than enough to allay any fears brought on through the most stubborn unbelief! However, there is another kind of fear that is highly effective at suppressing truth and that is the fear of man.

***The fear of man** bringeth a snare: but whoso putteth his trust in the LORD shall be safe.  (Proverbs 29:25)*

*I, even I, am he that comforteth you: who art thou, that thou shouldest be **afraid of a man** that shall die, and of the son of man which shall be made as grass;  (Isaiah 51:12)*

*Howbeit no man spake openly of him **for fear of the Jews**. (John 7:13)*

*Nevertheless among the chief rulers also many believed on him;* **but because of the Pharisees** *they did not confess him, lest they should be put out of the synagogue:* (John 12:42)

*For before that certain came from James, he did eat with the Gentiles: but when they were come, he withdrew and separated himself,* **fearing them which were of the circumcision.** (Galatians 2:12)

It would be difficult to quantify the proportion of error and disobedience within the Church that is traceable to 'the fear of man', but I believe that it is a very significant amount. The problem is not just a fear of men outside the professing church, but an undue fear of those within her bounds. In the verses just quoted, the last three involve what we might call 'fear of religious censure'.

The precious truth of the Gospel of God's salvation itself is now opposed within much of the church by many who call themselves Christians. Clearly, true believers must never allow a fear of being denounced by those of merely nominal Christian profession to prevent them proclaiming the truth. There is often no alternative for the faithful Christian but to separate themselves from churches and denominations that are falling headlong into the prophesied End-Time apostasy.

Yet it is when this principle is at work within the true Church that it can present a greater trial to the believer. We are to be *"Endeavouring to keep the unity of the Spirit in the bond of peace" (Ephesians 4:3)* and yet we are also to be *"Speaking the truth in love" (Ephesians 4:15a).* The Christian who loves the whole truth of God's Word quickly learns that, to share faithfully all that the Lord has taught him, he will sooner or later face opposition from some beloved brothers and sisters in Christ. This is painful and difficult because no one likes to be ill thought of by those they love and respect. This is when the temptation to suppress the truth can be very strong. However, the way *"to keep the unity of the Spirit in the bond of peace"* is not to suppress the truth but to *"speak the truth in love"*. This can be very costly and it is not uncommon for those who make such a stand to be asked to leave their fellowship. It was this fear that kept many of the 'chief rulers' quiet in John 12:42.

The secret to victory in all of this is a determination to seek to please God rather than men. Fear of the Lord will prevent the fear of man. In circumstances where we cannot have both, it is better to have the smile of God and the frown of beloved brothers and sisters, than to have the smile of brothers and sisters and the frown of God.

*For do I now persuade men, or God? or do I seek to please men? for **if I yet pleased men, I should not be the servant of Christ.*** *(Galatians 1:10)*

Perhaps you are saying to yourself that this is all very well, but I simply do not possess the boldness to stand alone over an important truth of God's Word. God can give you that boldness when He fills you with His Holy Spirit. In fact in today's Church, you will not be able to contend for the truth of the baptism with the Holy Spirit unless you yourself have received that baptism.

## CONCLUSION

We have seen that there are many different ways in which the truth of the baptism with the Holy Spirit is suppressed within much of the Church: error is 'corrected' with opposite error; good ministry constantly lacks an essential ingredient; study Bibles and commentaries are used uncritically; believers are wrongly taught that they were automatically baptised with the Holy Spirit at conversion; those who were once Spirit-filled shrink back under intimidation; some who believe in the promised baptism linger and fail to act on it; many have unwittingly opened the door to demonic interference through such occult practices as homoeopathy. Finally we looked at personal factors such as the influence of wrong teaching, pride, unbelief and fear. Some of these ways are subtle and others less so. Nevertheless, the remedy is the same in every instance, namely repentance, a return to the whole teaching and counsel of the Word of God and a ready obedience to it.

# CHAPTER 7

# DEALING WITH OBJECTIONS

### WE HAVE ALL BEEN BAPTISED WITH THE HOLY SPIRIT

From time to time, within cessationist assemblies, it is inevitable that a young believer will seek out an elder to ask about the baptism with the Holy Spirit. Perhaps they have heard about it from a Christian friend at school or college or read about it in some non-Brethren literature. The following verse has been misused many times to convince anxious enquirers that *all* believers have been baptised with the Holy Spirit.

***For by one Spirit are we all baptized into one body**, whether we be Jews or Gentiles, whether we be bond or free; and have been all made to drink into one Spirit. (1 Corinthians 12:13)*

It is really disappointing to witness those usually known for higher standards of Biblical exegesis trying to make this verse mean something that it does not. As long as we remember the triune nature of God, the true meaning of the verse becomes clear. It really boils down to this question: Who is baptising who and into what?

In the emboldened first part of the verse there are three

entities involved. These are the Holy Spirit *(one Spirit)*, the believer *(we all)* and the body of Christ *(one body)*. The verse is simply telling us that at our conversion the Holy Spirit baptises or places us into the body of Christ, the true Church. Note that it is the **Holy Spirit** who is doing the baptising, **we** who are being baptised and the **body of Christ**, the element into which we are being baptised. To help us further understand this, consider what happens when we are baptised in water. Again, there are three bodies involved. These are: the person who will baptise us (e.g. an elder), our self and the body of water. The elder baptises us in the water. Obviously we are not baptised with or into the elder but into the water. In like manner, in our verse we are not baptised with or into the Holy Spirit but into the body of Christ. Now contrast all this with the following statement by John the Baptist:

*I indeed baptize you with water unto repentance: but he that cometh after me is mightier than I, whose shoes I am not worthy to bear:* **he** (Jesus) **shall baptize you with the Holy Ghost,** *and with fire: (Matthew 3:11)*

Once again there are three entities involved. These are the Lord Jesus Christ, our self and the Holy Spirit. This time, it is the Lord Jesus Christ who is doing the baptising and not the Holy Spirit. One could say that it is the exact opposite of what is taking place in 1 Corinthians 12:13. In Matthew 3:11, it is said that the Lord Jesus Christ will baptise us with or into the Holy Spirit. This is the baptism with the Holy Spirit and must not be confused with what takes place at our conversion as described in 1 Corinthians 12:13.

Another closely related objection is based on the following verse:

*Blessed be the God and Father of our Lord Jesus Christ,* **who hath blessed us with all spiritual blessings** *in heavenly places in Christ:* (Ephesians 1:3)

Some believers reason from this verse that since they are already *"blessed... with all spiritual blessings"* there can be nothing else to seek from God. At first this might seem a plausible argument, but it does not bear a close examination. Take the following verse from the book of James that was written to believers:

*If any of you* **lack wisdom,** *let him ask of God, that giveth to all men liberally, and upbraideth not; and it shall be given him.* (James 1:5)

Using the same logic, the above verse should not be necessary since, how could any believer *"lack wisdom"* if he is already *"blessed... with all spiritual blessings"*? The wisdom being spoken about is not worldly, but heavenly and is therefore a spiritual blessing. At first this might seem a quandary, but it is not really. The spiritual blessings being spoken of are often in the form of promises to believers that God has made in His Word. James 1:5 teaches that it is entirely possible for a believer to lack wisdom. If he recognises his deficiency, the spiritual blessing consists of free access to God to ask for wisdom with the certainty that it shall be given to him. It is the same with the baptism with the Holy Spirit, which is a promise of God for all believers. If you are conscious that you have never been baptised with the Holy Spirit and endued with a spiritual gift or gifts, you have but to ask your Heavenly Father in simple faith and you will receive what you seek.

C H Spurgeon well understood this principle. One of his best-known daily devotionals is called the "Cheque Book of the Bank of Faith" in which he says the following as part of the preface:

*"A **promise** from God may very instructively be compared to a cheque payable to order. It is given to the believer with the view of bestowing upon him some good thing. It is not meant that he should read it over comfortably, and then have done with it. No, he is to treat the promise as a reality, as a man treats a cheque."*

If we were to receive a cheque for a large amount of money, it would be rather foolish to file it away and then go out and try to spend the money. No, we would first note whether the sender of the cheque was bona fide and then go to our bank to present it. We would present it in faith, not doubting for a minute that the money would clear into our account. Having checked our new account balance, only then would we venture to go out and spend the money.

In his "Morning by Morning" devotional for July 27, Spurgeon penned some further helpful thoughts on the following scripture:

*Exceeding great and precious promises (extract from 2 Peter 1:4)*

*"If you would know experimentally the preciousness of the promises, and enjoy them in your own heart, meditate much upon them. There are promises which are like grapes in the wine-press; if you will tread them the juice will flow. Thinking over the hallowed words will often be the prelude to their fulfilment. While you are musing upon them, the boon which*

*you are seeking will insensibly come to you. Many a Christian who has thirsted for the promise has found the favour which it ensured gently distilling into his soul even while he has been considering the divine record; and he has rejoiced that ever he was led to lay the promise near his heart."*

Let us not confuse God's various promises to us as believers with our salvation, which is complete and needs nothing adding to it.

## I WAS TOLD THAT I DO NOT HAVE THE HOLY SPIRIT

Ironically, more harm is sometimes done to the teaching of the baptism with the Holy Spirit by its friends than its enemies. This can happen when (typically) a relatively new believer, who is not yet well instructed in the Word, is baptised with the Holy Spirit. Perceiving the difference that it has made, they imply that their Christian friends, who have not had the same experience, do not have the Holy Spirit. This is not only hurtful to them, but also untrue. As we saw in chapter 3, it is clear that **all** true believers are indwelt with and sealed with the Holy Spirit.

*But ye are not in the flesh, but in the Spirit, if so be that the Spirit of God dwell in you.* ***Now if any man have not the Spirit of Christ, he is none of his.*** *(Romans 8:9)*

*In whom ye also trusted, after that ye heard the word of truth, the gospel of your salvation: in whom also **after that ye believed, ye were sealed with that holy Spirit of promise,*** *(Ephesians 1:13)*

We also saw that there is a very wide difference between being indwelt and sealed with the Holy Spirit and being filled with the power of the Holy Spirit. Just because someone has been baptised with the Holy Spirit, he or she does not instantly become a skilful expositor of the doctrine from the Scriptures. If erroneous statements are made, these are sometimes seized upon by cessationists to discredit the teaching. This is another example of employing a 'straw man' argument that we looked at in chapter 6. We should not really be surprised by this as a similar principle was at work when the man born blind was healed by the Lord Jesus in John's Gospel, chapter 9. When he was brought before the Pharisees to give an account of what had happened, he was able to tell them little more than the Name of the Man who had restored his sight. The Pharisees sought to take advantage of the man's lack of knowledge but were ultimately confounded upon being confronted with such an evident token of Jesus' Messiahship. Clearly, it behoves us all who have been baptised with the Holy Spirit to try and gain a scriptural understanding of the underlying doctrine so that we are able to explain it to others.


## THE BIBLE TEACHES THAT PROPHECIES AND TONGUES WILL CEASE

This statement is true as we shall see in the following verses. The big question, however, is precisely *when* they will cease.


*(1 Corinthians 13:8) Charity never faileth: but whether there be prophecies, they shall fail; whether there be tongues, they shall cease; whether there be knowledge, it shall vanish away.*

*(1 Corinthians 13:9) For we know in part, and we prophesy in part.*

*(1 Corinthians 13:10)  But **WHEN** that which is perfect is come,* then *that which is in part shall be done away.*

*(1 Corinthians 13:11)  When I was a child, I spake as a child, I understood as a child, I thought as a child: but when I became a man, I put away childish things.*

*(1 Corinthians 13:12)  For **<u>now</u>** we see through a glass, darkly; but **THEN** face to face: **<u>now</u>** I know in part; but **THEN** shall I know even as also I am known.*

Certain words have been emboldened and either capitalised or underlined in the preceding passage for reasons that will become apparent shortly.

Many cessationists appeal to this passage to try and prove that prophecies and tongues have ceased. To do this they need to define what is meant by the phrase, *"when that which is perfect is come"* in verse 10. Ingeniously, they assert that it is referring to the point in time when the Scriptures were completed with the finishing of the New Testament. They correctly argue that the Scriptures can be rightly described as, *"that which is perfect"*. Thus they conclude that prophecies and tongues must have ceased because we have the Bible, which is the completed Canon of Scripture. Yet there are major problems with this interpretation.

Firstly, the whole context of the passage has nothing to do with the writing of the Scriptures or their completion. Secondly, if Paul had meant us to understand that he was referring to the completion of Scripture, he could have stated so very plainly and unambiguously, especially when such an important doctrinal matter hinged upon such a statement. Thirdly, the conclusion of the matter in verse 12 makes no sense at all if verse 10 referred to the completion of the Scriptures.

The passage refers to two different points in time; firstly the time at which Paul was writing and secondly a future time *"when that which is perfect is come"*. In our passage, the time at which Paul was writing is twice referred to in verse 12 by the word *"__now__"*. The future time is referred to in verse 10 by the word *"WHEN"* and twice more in verse 12 with the word *"THEN"*.

To help us see clearly whether Paul meant us to understand his phrase, *"when that which is perfect is come"*, to mean the completion of Scripture, we will reproduce the passage. This time though, we will substitute for the word *"__now__"* the phrase, "Before the Scriptures are complete". Likewise we will substitute for the words *"WHEN that which is perfect is come"* and *"THEN"* the phrase, "After the Scriptures are complete".

*(1 Corinthians 13:8) Charity never faileth: but whether there be prophecies, they shall fail; whether there be tongues, they shall cease; whether there be knowledge, it shall vanish away.*

*(1 Corinthians 13:9)* For we know in part, and we prophesy in part.

*(1 Corinthians 13:10) But **after the Scriptures are complete**, then that which is in part shall be done away.*

*(1 Corinthians 13:11) When I was a child, I spake as a child, I understood as a child, I thought as a child: but when I became a man, I put away childish things.*

*(1 Corinthians 13:12) For **before the Scriptures are complete** we see through a glass, darkly; but **after the Scriptures are complete** face to face: **before the Scriptures are complete** I know in part; but **after the Scriptures are complete** shall I know even as also I am known.*

The whole matter hinges on verse 12. Now that we have

the complete Bible, we need only to ask whether we now see *"face to face"* and *"know even as also we are known"*. Clearly, we do not. Therefore *"that which is perfect"* cannot possibly refer to the Canon of Scripture being completed. It can only refer to that wonderful time, soon to come, when we shall be in the presence of the Lord Jesus Christ in God's kingdom. Obviously, there will be no need for prophecies, tongues or any other such gifts then!

## THERE ARE TOO MANY COUNTERFEIT SPIRITUAL MANIFESTATIONS

Money is counterfeited and so are expensive watches, but have you ever heard of a problem with counterfeit paper bags? Obviously counterfeiters only bother to make fake copies of that which has real value. The existence of a counterfeit also points to the existence of that which is genuine; it would be impossible to counterfeit something which did not exist. When did you last see people afraid to withdraw money from a cash machine because of the existence of counterfeit currency?

Likewise in the spiritual realm: Satan only counterfeits that which is real and valuable, obviously not for the purpose of financial gain but rather to cause confusion and bring the truth into disrepute. Sadly he has been very successful with this ploy, deceiving multitudes of professing Christians with spurious manifestations, often through Christendom's equivalent of snake oil salesmen (who *are* in it for financial gain). Many correctly point out that where the Bible mentions signs and wonders in the context of the very last days, they are invariably of the false variety, as the following verse indicates:

*Even him, whose coming is after the working of Satan with all power and signs and lying wonders, (2 Thessalonians 2:9)*

Particularly rational and careful thinking is required here. As we saw in chapter 6, there is a great danger of trying to correct error with error. Does the fact that we are living at the end of the present age and witnessing many counterfeit signs and wonders mean that there are no genuine gifts of the Holy Spirit? Clearly this is an illogical conclusion, prompted more by fear of the false than by careful scriptural reasoning. Further to this, if cessationists are correct that the gifts of the Holy Spirit were withdrawn when the Canon of Scripture was completed and therefore do not exist in the present, then there can be no such thing as counterfeit signs and wonders. Why do I say this? Simply because there can only be a counterfeit of something that actually exists. The following verses instruct us in the proper way to discern between the true and the false:

*(1 Thessalonians 5:19)  Quench not the Spirit.*
*(1 Thessalonians 5:20)  Despise not prophesyings.*
*(1 Thessalonians 5:21)  **Prove all things**; hold fast that which is good.*

We "prove all things" by testing them against the teaching of the Word of God.


## THE CORINTHIANS WERE CARNAL

Why are the Corinthians often used as a reason to avoid the subject of spiritual gifts? Obviously the book of 1 Corinthians contains the most extensive instruction concerning the supernatural gifts of the Holy Spirit. Paul's letter was occasioned, among other things, by their excitement with, and frequent misuse of, spiritual gifts. He had to rebuke them for being carnal, which showed itself in their internal divisions, unjudged sin and disorders at the Lord's table. Too often Christians point a rather self-righteous finger at the Corinthians, relieved that their own assembly is so 'respectable' and nothing like that at Corinth. Yet what they fail to see is that their own assembly does not possess the *life* that the Corinthians had.

A preacher once used the illustration of a nursery school full of spirited young children. Their vibrant life manifests itself in much noise and activity that, due to their immaturity, requires skilful and sympathetic supervision by adults. If the children possess none of that spirit, we can only imagine the dismal scene as they sit around in lethargic inactivity. One would have to conclude that there is something seriously wrong with them in such a case. It would certainly make the job of the adult supervisors much easier, as there would be no noise, no excesses, no friction between children and indeed no anything! Clearly nobody would desire such a state of affairs. For this reason a good nursery school teacher will not seek to stifle the spirit of the children, but rather guide and direct it to purposeful ends. The preacher went on to apply the analogy to the Church. He said that you only have problems where there is *life*; anyone can keep order in a cemetery!

Of course the life the preacher was referring to is that produced by the energy of the Holy Spirit, filling and equipping the believers with varying gifts. It was not that depressing substitute for the genuine, namely, carefully choreographed meetings where everything is under the control of men. Doubtless there is less of a challenge for leaders in such meetings, but that is no excuse for the sin of quenching the Spirit.

## THE HOLY SPIRIT DOES NOT SPEAK ABOUT HIMSELF

This objection comes from a wrong understanding of the following verse:

*Howbeit when he, the Spirit of truth, is come, he will guide you into all truth: **for he shall not speak of himself**; but whatsoever he shall hear, that shall he speak: and he will shew you things to come.* (John 16:13)

We should note that a part of the above verse is often misused by those who think it wrong to spend time teaching about the Holy Spirit. Where our Lord Jesus says, *"for He shall not speak of Himself"*, they wrongly conclude that the Holy Spirit never speaks about Himself. What it actually means is that the Holy Spirit never speaks on His own authority, but speaks only those things that He receives from the Father and the Son. During His earthly ministry, the Lord Jesus was exactly the same; He spoke only those things that came from His Father. Did this mean that He never spoke about Himself? Of course not. The principal object of the Holy Spirit is always to glorify the Lord Jesus Christ. Nevertheless, we must remember that the Lord Jesus taught much about the Holy Spirit, who is mentioned a very large number of times throughout the rest of the New Testament. Since the Holy Spirit is the author of the Scriptures, He necessarily has to mention Himself.

## THIS TEACHING CAN CAUSE DIVISION

Truth always brings division. The truth of the Gospel itself brings division between merely nominal Christians and those who have been born of the Spirit of God through personal faith in the Lord Jesus Christ. The truth about creation brings division between those who uphold the Word of God and those who have compromised with the world's philosophy of evolution. The truth about God's purposes for Israel as distinct from the Church brings division between those who take His Word at face value and those who spiritualise the Scriptures and claim that the Church has replaced Israel. One could add many more instances of truth bringing division from falsehood, but these will suffice to make the point.

The question we must ask is this: Who does the Bible hold responsible for bringing division into the Church? Is it those who insist on upholding the truth or those who suppress it? On one occasion the following words were quoted to a brother who was warning believers in his locality about the true nature of a well-known spiritual deception that many of them were imbibing in the 1990s:

*"Mark them which cause divisions and offences and avoid them."*

This misquote of Romans 16:17 was intended to imply that the brother bringing the warning was guilty of causing divisions and offences and should therefore be avoided. Here is what the verse actually says:

*Now I beseech you, brethren, mark them which cause divisions and offences **contrary to the doctrine which ye have learned**; and avoid them.* (Romans 16:17)

Notice the words in bold, which make all the difference to our understanding of just who is responsible for divisions and offences within the Church. It is those who either suppress true doctrine or introduce false doctrine that the Word of God holds responsible for the mischief.

## First and Second Class Christians?

It is often objected that this teaching divides the Body of Christ into first and second class Christians. To answer this we need to think biblically about all that we have and are. Our talents and gifting all come from God, therefore none of us has anything to boast about or to give rise to pride.

*For who maketh thee to differ from another? and what hast thou that thou didst not receive? now if thou didst receive it, why dost thou glory, as if thou hadst not received it?*
(1 Corinthians 4:7)

Analogies have their limitations, but I offer this one that might be helpful in understanding the principle involved:

Imagine a large group of young men newly recruited into the Army. After completing all of the formalities they are individually sworn in at their attestation. They are now officially in the Army and all of them are therefore soldiers. Imagine that the word went round that they should all now report to the quartermaster's store to be issued with various items of essential equipment. However some of the group were not present when that edict was given and therefore did not collect their equipment. On the first full day of practical training, some of the group were properly equipped and the rest were not.

Were they all still soldiers? Of course. Were the equipped soldiers any better *in themselves* than their non-equipped colleagues? Of course not. Were the equipped soldiers more effective with the training mission than their non-equipped colleagues? Definitely.

In this analogy it is obvious that the non-equipped soldiers would soon realise their error. They would hardly be likely to complain that their equipped colleagues were guilty of making them feel like second-class soldiers. Instead, they would go to the quartermaster's store to collect their equipment at the first opportunity.

In the matter of the baptism with the Holy Spirit, Christians might not have received it for the same reason that our soldiers had not received their equipment, namely that they have not heard that they should receive it. However, this is where a difference occurs. Once the soldiers realised they were not equipped, they went straight to the quartermaster to rectify the situation. Can we imagine any of them refusing to go or refusing to believe that there was any equipment for them in the store? Yet this is precisely what many Christians do after learning that there is such a thing as the baptism with the Holy Spirit to receive.

The question as to whether it creates first and second class Christians is therefore the same as in our analogy with the soldiers; it does not. The problem is largely due to those Christians who are determined *not* to seek God for this baptism and who wish to portray their position as standard Christianity. From that position it becomes all too easy to blame those who have been baptised with the Holy Spirit, and who contend for the truth of it, for supposedly creating a two-tier Church of first and second class Christians.


## WE ARE TOO NEAR THE END OF THE AGE


This objection needs to be looked at very carefully. This author firmly believes that we are living in the closing days of this present age. Not only that, but I am also strongly persuaded that the coming of the Lord Jesus Christ for His Church, in what is known as the Rapture, is imminent. By imminent I mean that no specific prophecy of the Scriptures needs to be fulfilled before that event, which necessarily means that it will occur before the soon to dawn seven-year Tribulation period. I believe this view to be the most consistent with the New Testament scriptures and in harmony with Old Testament typology. Interestingly, amongst the varying views, it is the one that attracts by far the most bitter and venomous attacks from within the professing church. Surely, this also points to the strong likelihood that the pre-Tribulation Rapture is the correct understanding of the Scriptures. It is not my intention to enlarge on that blessed hope here, as it has been very ably taught and written about by godly and scholarly men from yesteryear, as well as many of the most gifted and respected Bible teachers of our day.

Why have I taken time to declare my convictions about these things? It is because many brothers and sisters who share the same view believe that because things in the Church and Nation have sunk so low, there is no hope of another outpouring of the Holy Spirit upon believers bringing revival in the true Church. They correctly point out that the whole thrust of the prophetic Scriptures teaches that there will be a 'falling away' or apostasy, false teaching and spiritual deception on a grand scale within the professing church as we near the return of the Lord Jesus Christ. Further to this, the nations will be in moral free-fall, casting off restraint and legalising that which God says He abhors. These are exactly the conditions prevailing in 2014 that, together with international 'land for peace' pressure upon Israel and an exponential increase in 'natural' disaster frequency,  reliably indicate that time is very short indeed.  As a result of all this, many Christians conclude that there cannot possibly be a revival.

Before going any further, we should define precisely what we mean by 'revival'. Many have a wrong idea that it simply means multitudes of people being saved. As a result of past well-documented revivals, there have usually been significant numbers of people saved. However, revival primarily concerns those who are already Christians. You cannot revive something which has never had life in the first place. An unbeliever has never had spiritual life and therefore needs saving, not reviving. On the other hand, believers and the wider true Church can sadly sink into a very spiritually moribund state, as is all too common in Britain today. In such a case the only remedy is a Heaven-sent revival.

There is a tendency to think of revival as extraordinary and even spectacular. Yet this is only because the results are in such dramatic contrast with the spiritually decayed condition of the Church. God's purpose in sending revival is simply to lift the Church back up to a level from which she should never have fallen. Put simply, if the Church in the West does not resemble that described in the Book of Acts, she ought to be on her knees praying to God for revival.

Another completely wrong notion about revival is to equate it with 'charismania' and the false and dangerous teaching that the Church will become more and more impressive and influential, thus enabling her to 'Christianise' the world prior to the return of the Lord Jesus Christ. Even a modest understanding of the general thrust of Bible prophecy concerning the 'End Times' and an un-blinkered look at what is actually happening in the world would prevent such a deceptive belief.

Let us be quite clear; the Bible does not teach that there *must* be a revival before the Rapture of the Church. On the contrary, it teaches that most of the professing church will be immersed in false teaching and outright apostasy when the Lord Jesus appears. Does this therefore mean that there *cannot* be a revival in a particular location or country before He returns? Looking at the prevailing conditions of apostasy and the apparent shortness of time left, many answer 'yes'. However, we need to remember just Who it is that controls the timetable of events in this world. It is the sovereign God of the universe, who does not have a timeframe imposed upon Him by others.

At the time of writing this paragraph, events and trends around the world are far advanced in setting the stage for the earth-shattering fulfilment of Biblical prophecies soon to take place. With these events already on the horizon for those with eyes to see, how much nearer still must the Rapture of the Church be? Yet God alone knows precisely when it will take place; it could be only days away (or even today) or there might be a couple of years or more to go. Therefore, are we being scripturally correct to assert that there *cannot* be a revival before the Rapture? The answer to this must be no. Conversely, are we being scripturally correct to assert that there *must* be a revival before the Rapture? Again, the answer must be no.

I believe the only scriptural conclusion we can come to is that God alone will determine whether or not He revives the Church in Britain before He sends His well-beloved Son, the Lord Jesus Christ, to catch away His waiting bride at the Rapture. So, should we be praying for revival? In chapter 1 we sought to 'diagnose the need' for revival and demonstrated how desperately the Church in Britain and the West in general needs it. Therefore if we desire to see God glorified in His Church and what would very probably be the last ingathering of unsaved sinners, we should be praying earnestly for revival.

Yet let us remember that whether or not God grants revival in a general sense, He will most certainly fulfil His promise to baptise with the Holy Spirit those believers who ask Him in faith. Such individuals will experience personal revival. They will doubtless find that God does much more through them in the short period remaining than they had done for God in the entire time since their salvation.

## CONCLUSION

We have looked at several common objections to the baptism with the Holy Spirit as distinct from conversion. These range from confusion caused by misinterpreting or misapplying Scripture, to honest concerns about division and to a belief that things are too far gone to be able to hope for revival. It is my prayer that the answers given to these objections will help readers to see that it is right for believers to ask God for the baptism with the Holy Spirit and to pray for revival in the Church.

# CHAPTER 8

# CLOSING THOUGHTS

## CAN OUTSIDERS TELL THE DIFFERENCE BETWEEN US AND JEHOVAH'S WITNESSES?

This is a very interesting and challenging question. As Bible believing Christians, we know that there is a world of difference between a blood-bought child of God, saved by grace, and one who is sincerely, but mistakenly, trying to earn their salvation in a pseudo-Christian cult such as the Jehovah's Witnesses (JWs). The question is not whether *we* can see the difference, but whether outsiders can see the difference. These days the majority of unbelievers have no idea of the vital difference between the Biblical Gospel of salvation and what is taught by groups such as the JWs.

JWs are often very kind and friendly. They are ready to spend time with people, answering their questions and giving them free literature. To the unwary they can seem just like genuine Christians. As a matter of fact, their zeal sometimes puts us to shame. As we arrive at our meeting places and JWs arrive at theirs, is there any real difference as far as those outside are concerned? Indeed, how are they to know the difference?

The true Christian is indwelt with the Holy Spirit and as such will confess the truth about the person of the Lord Jesus Christ, His deity as well as His perfect manhood. Yet this is not an obvious distinguishing feature from the point of view of those outside. However, the Christian has the potential to be baptised with the Holy Spirit after which *"rivers of living water"* should flow out from his inmost being to those around. When this happens to all within an assembly the result is revival. Well-documented accounts of historic revivals clearly indicate that a revived Church has a dramatic effect upon those outside. Many sense that God is truly among His people, come under conviction of their own sin and hasten to the meetings to hear how they might be saved from the coming judgement.

A genuine revival can only take place amongst God's people, the true Church. This is made up of every man, woman and child who has been born anew by the regenerating power of God's Spirit. They alone have a living faith in the Lord Jesus Christ and are indwelt by the Holy Spirit. Only they can be *"endued with power from on high"* if and when they are baptised with the Holy Spirit. We pointed out in chapter 5 that there has never been an authentic revival within the Roman Catholic Church, the JWs or in any other of the multitude of pseudo-Christian false religious systems. The reason for this is simple; none of those systems are the work of the Holy Spirit, therefore not one of them represents the true Church of God on earth. Every one of them can be shown to be false by making a simple comparison of their teachings with the Word of God. We should point out here that, by the grace of God, a tiny minority do get saved within these false systems if and when the Holy Spirit opens their eyes to the truth as it is in the Bible. As these new converts continue to study the Scriptures they would read the following verses:

*(2 Corinthians 6:14) Be ye not unequally yoked together with unbelievers: for what fellowship hath righteousness with unrighteousness? and what communion hath light with darkness?*

*(2 Corinthians 6:15) And what concord hath Christ with Belial? or what part hath he that believeth with an infidel?*

*(2 Corinthians 6:16) And what agreement hath the temple of God with idols? for ye are the temple of the living God; as God hath said, I will dwell in them, and walk in them; and I will be their God, and they shall be my people.*

*(2 Corinthians 6:17)* **Wherefore come out from among them, and be ye separate,** *saith the Lord, and touch not the unclean thing; and I will receive you,*

*(2 Corinthians 6:18) And will be a Father unto you, and ye shall be my sons and daughters, saith the Lord Almighty.*

This passage teaches that God would have His people separate themselves from being intrinsically linked in relationships or associations with that which He cannot own. This means that a believer should not be joined with unbelievers in the sense of participating in their sinful pleasures. It also means that a believer should not marry an unbeliever (the case of one party being saved after marriage is completely different and is dealt with in 1 Corinthians 7:12-16).

However, the teaching that is most pertinent to our subject is that of separating from false religious systems. Some who come to know the Lord whilst in a counterfeit religious organisation remain part of it, believing that they can reform it or at least influence it in some degree. The track record of success in such endeavours is dismal indeed. The scriptural teaching for believers is to separate themselves from false systems and join together with those who are known to be true Christians. If all believers obeyed this principle, 'clear blue water' would more readily be seen between the true and the false. How Satan loves a mixture and labours to achieve it wherever he can. It is thus that he too often succeeds in obscuring clear Gospel witness. These things will all come to a climactic head as the soon-coming Tribulation period closes this present age. Temporarily dominating this time will be a grotesque amalgamation of the Roman Catholic Church, Islam, apostate Protestant denominations and every other world religion, which will form the one world religion referred to in the Book of Revelation as *"MYSTERY, BABYLON THE GREAT, THE MOTHER OF HARLOTS AND ABOMINATIONS OF THE EARTH" (Revelation 17:5).* It is clear from the Scriptures that after the true Church has been removed to Heaven at the Rapture, there will be many people saved during the terrible Tribulation period. These are known as Tribulation saints. As regards their relationship with the false one world 'church' that will then be in existence, God instructs them in no uncertain terms:

*And I heard another voice from heaven, saying,* **Come out of her, my people,** *that ye be not partakers of her sins, and that ye receive not of her plagues. (Revelation 18:4)*

How graciously God warns His true children to separate themselves from that abominable religious system that He is about to judge just four verses later.

***Therefore shall her plagues come in one day,*** *death, and mourning, and famine; and she shall be utterly burned with fire:* ***for strong is the Lord God who judgeth her.*** *(Revelation 18:8)*

Let us reiterate here that the Biblical principle of separation from false religious systems and formerly sound churches that have 'gone off the rails' applies here and now and not just in the coming Tribulation period. If God is to grant revival for a short season, there will first have to be something of repentance and reformation among believers. We will have to take seriously the command to be separate from false religion and stop making excuses for staying within it. Churches that are not guilty in that respect but have quenched the Holy Spirit with cessationist or similar teaching will also need to repent before God.

We started this chapter asking whether outsiders could tell the difference between true Christians and JWs. With the current spiritual state of the Church in Britain, we have to conclude that 'the man on the street' would have a hard time telling the difference. Would he have a similar difficulty in telling the difference between the Church as described in the Book of Acts and the JWs? Clearly, there would be no difficulty at all in that case, but for what reason? Is it not because those early Christians were all filled with the Holy Spirit and God was so clearly in their midst enabling them to do great exploits for His Kingdom?

What is our response to this? Do we just shrug our shoulders and say, "that was then, but this is now"? If we do, then assuredly our soul is not in a healthy state. If, on the other hand, we are stirred to godly sorrow over the matter, there is more than a little hope that God will hear and answer our tears of repentance and prayer for the baptism with His Holy Spirit.

## WARNINGS

It is very important to understand that this book is written for people who have already been saved. I have deliberately used the Biblical word 'saved' rather than 'made a decision for Christ', 'come to Christ', 'come to faith' or other similar phrases. This is because we need to define precisely what makes the difference between a person whom God has saved and one who has merely taken the name of 'Christian' after completing some course, joining a church, repeating the 'sinners prayer' or signing a decision card. In these days of confusion and widespread false teaching in the professing church, the 'gospel' preached is often hopelessly inadequate to bring a genuine conviction of sin to the hearer. Too often, ears are tickled and self is pandered to in order to get people into the church. Such people are told that they have become Christians, often in the complete absence of any evidence of a deep conviction of their sin and the repentance that should follow. If sin is mentioned at all, it is only as it affects the person, in terms of unpleasant consequences they have experienced, rather than the grievous offence that it is to a holy God. The truth that they are sinners from birth, are under the righteous wrath of God and, unless they repent, are on their way to an everlasting Hell is usually missing. The hearers of this false 'gospel' are left with no urgent sense that they need to *"flee from the wrath to come"*.

*Then said he to the multitude that came forth to be baptized of him, O generation of vipers, who hath warned you to **flee from the wrath to come?*** *(Luke 3:7)*

It is a vital part of the ministry of the Holy Spirit to convict and convince unbelievers of their sin and rebellion against God, of God's righteousness and of certain judgement to come.

*And when he is come, he will reprove* (convict/convince) *the world of sin, and of righteousness, and of judgment:*
(John 16:8)

## The Alpha Course

Much has been written to warn of the shortcomings and dangers of the hugely popular Alpha Course, therefore I do not intend to go into great detail here. Nevertheless, it has become a very significant phenomenon in Western Christianity and so it needs to be mentioned, particularly as it relates to the subject of this book.

One can readily see the appeal of such a course to so many churches that have experienced dwindling congregations for many years. The 'Alpha' brand name seems to hold out the promise of rejuvenation in terms of both numbers and spiritual condition. On the other hand, many discerning Christian writers have put the Alpha Course under the microscope and concluded that 'not all that glitters is gold'.

If the Church was what it should be, one has to ask why such a course is deemed necessary. After all, God has promised to save sinners through the agency of preaching.

*For after that in the wisdom of God the world by wisdom knew not God, it pleased God by the foolishness of preaching to save them that believe. (1 Corinthians 1:21)*

What needs to be preached if we expect to see God fulfilling His promise? It is certainly not the watered down, so-called seeker sensitive 'gospel' presented on the average Alpha Course. Such compromise is the inevitable result of having abandoned confidence in the veracity of *the whole of* God's Word many years ago. A generation brainwashed by evolution, surely the greatest deception in modern times, first needs to be authoritatively challenged with the truth of God as Creator from the Scriptures. The apostle Paul used this approach when dealing with the Athenians who, unlike the Jews, had no foundational understanding of God as Creator of all things (Acts 17:18-34). Likewise, due to evolutionary indoctrination, today's generation has largely lost any understanding that there is a Creator God. Then the fact of universal sin having its origin in the fall of man, as recorded in Genesis chapter 3, must be explained. The proof of indwelling sin must be pointed out; this lies in the fact that we have all broken God's laws and cannot perfectly keep them even supposing we wanted to. These foundational truths are essential to a correct understanding of the reason why the Lord Jesus Christ laid down His life on that cruel cross nearly 2000 years ago. As the only perfect and sinless Man, He alone could pay the penalty of sin, which is death, on behalf of all who confess and forsake their sin and place their whole trust in Him, His death and resurrection on their behalf as their sole hope of salvation.

*For he* (God the Father) *hath made him* (Jesus the Son) *to be sin for us, who knew no sin; that we might be made the righteousness of God in him.* (2 Corinthians 5:21)

Does the Alpha 'gospel' confront men and women with their true position before God with sufficient accuracy and potency to bring genuine conviction of sin? Sadly, the answer has to be no. Does this mean that no one is ever saved on an Alpha Course? There will always be a small number obtaining genuine, saving faith in the midst of prevailing compromise and error. However, this fact no more validates the Alpha Course than a Catholic being saved legitimises the Roman Catholic Church. Wherever the grace of God is at work in a human heart, they are led to the true Gospel, either by reading it in the Bible for themselves or having it explained by a faithful witness. In such cases we might say that God in His grace saves some *despite* surrounding spiritual influences, rather than *because* of them.

So why do we mention the Alpha Course in connection with the subject of this book, the baptism with the Holy Spirit? We have tried to show throughout this book that the baptism with the Holy Spirit is only for those who are *already* saved. It is an equipping for service for those who have already been set apart for God by the new birth. After an inadequate explanation of the Gospel in talk three of the Alpha Course, the rest of the programme more or less assumes that the attendees have become Christians. This is a dangerous presumption, particularly when it comes to the 'weekend away', sometimes known as the 'Holy Spirit Weekend'. The purpose of the weekend is to introduce people to the Holy Spirit and that they might be filled or baptised with the Holy Spirit. The probability is that the majority of the attendees, if not all of them, are not genuinely converted. There are many reports of various spiritual manifestations on these weekends. These range from feelings of 'love' and 'joy' to quite bizarre physical displays such as shaking or uncontrollable laughter. Outlandish manifestations are clearly not of the Holy Spirit, since He is a God of order. Further to this, an important part of the fruit of the Holy Spirit in a believer's life is self-control (Galatians 5:23). But what can we say about pleasant feelings such as 'love', 'joy' and 'peace'? We must realise from the teaching of the Scriptures that the Holy Spirit will not give a wonderful sense of love and joy unless He has first convicted a person of their sin and rebellion against God. That process can be rather unpleasant as we are brought face-to-face with what we really are in the sight of a holy God. If by His grace we are led to confess our sin and repent of it and look by faith to the Lord Jesus Christ to save us, then and only then will we know that genuine joy and peace that comes from knowing sins forgiven. So if unregenerate (i.e. unsaved) people are experiencing spiritual manifestations, who or what is giving them?

*(2 Corinthians 11:3) But I fear, lest by any means, as the serpent beguiled Eve through his subtilty, so your minds should be corrupted from the simplicity that is in Christ.*

*(2 Corinthians 11:4) For if he that cometh preacheth **another Jesus**, whom we have not preached, or if ye receive **another spirit**, which ye have not received, or **another gospel**, which ye have not accepted, ye might well bear with him.*

*And no marvel; for **Satan himself is transformed into an angel of light**. (2 Corinthians 11:14)*

Satan is very happy with any religious programme that either bypasses or minimises the fact of sin and its origin in Adam that made necessary the cross of the Lord Jesus Christ. He has been in the business of planting false 'believers' within the professing church since the beginning. The Lord Jesus taught this important truth in the parable of the 'wheat and tares' (Matthew 13:24-30). When did you last hear this passage faithfully expounded from the pulpit?

Do not be fooled by the apparent success of the Alpha Course. The fact that the Roman Catholic Church has embraced it should ring loud alarm bells for all those who desire to remain faithful to God's Word. The Alpha Course is undoubtedly a powerful vehicle for promoting the worldwide Ecumenical Movement.

## The Ecumenical Movement

Multitudes of professing Christians, including some who are no doubt true Christians, are enthusiastically involved with the ecumenical movement; but what is the ecumenical movement? In a nutshell, it aims to bring together all the different Christian denominations in a visible show of unity. What could possibly be wrong with that? To non-Christians and professing Christians who do not know their Bibles, it seems like a very noble aim. The big problem is that it becomes a 'unity' based on the lowest common denominator. If necessary (and it *is* necessary), vital Biblical doctrines are abandoned in order to achieve an acceptable consensus. The result is a 'unity' based on a man-made compromise rather than on the truth of God's Word. Thus what is created is not the Church that the Lord Jesus Christ is building, but a false church. The World Council of Churches (WCC) avidly promotes the ecumenical movement and has for many years been conducting a courtship with the Roman Catholic Church. At a local level, the process has been advanced through 'Churches Together' partnerships or similar. Ecumenism has accelerated rapidly in recent years and now involves even evangelical churches, some of which are ready to compromise with Rome's false gospel. It is not difficult to see that the ultimate destination of the ecumenical movement is a one world 'church' under Rome. The coming into being of a one world 'church' is clearly prophesied in the Bible for the end of this present age. We should take serious note of how God describes this all-embracing religious system when considering whether to remain within a church whose leadership is sympathetic to, or has already embarked on, the ecumenical road:

*And upon her forehead was a name written, MYSTERY, BABYLON THE GREAT, THE MOTHER OF HARLOTS AND ABOMINATIONS OF THE EARTH.* (Revelation 17:5)

## The Charismatic Movement

It would be impossible in this short section to deal with every aspect of what has become known as the charismatic movement. Instead, some of the factors relevant to our case will be identified.

Most are agreed that the modern charismatic movement began in the 1960s. Originally, the word 'charismatic' simply described those Christians who believed that the gifts (or charismata) of the Holy Spirit are still available today and therefore they rejected the unscriptural dogma of cessationism. It began to be described as a 'movement' as more and more like-minded believers were drawn together, often forming new fellowships. Some remained in their existing denominations and became the 'charismatics within'. Many of the new fellowships started out very Biblically sound, with mature and godly men in the leadership. However, something has gone very badly wrong. How and why has this happened?

The answer is simple: departure from the Word of God. As many became more interested in experiences than sound doctrine, deceptive teaching and spurious practices gained an entrance. This trend has accelerated over the decades to the extent that the very word 'charismatic' has now become synonymous with the worst kinds of End Time deception. Money and 'Faith' preachers, disreputable televangelists and religious charlatans of every shade now come under the general description of 'charismatic'. Thus a perfectly valid and Biblical word now sends shudders through the majority of those who love the truth of God's Word. The same principle is in operation with the word 'evangelical'. In the past, an evangelical was somebody who had been genuinely converted through the new birth and whose faith and practice was governed solely by the Scriptures. Today, due to the heretical and apostate teachings of high-profile evangelicals and their ready compromise with the Roman Catholic Church, the word is becoming increasingly meaningless. At the time of writing, it is reported that there is phenomenal growth in what are called Pentecostal churches in various parts of the world and even revival at one church in the UK. The word 'Pentecostal' now seems to be misused to describe any church in which there is a loud, pop music style of 'worship' and much emotionalism. Modern 'revivals' frequently lay a tremendous emphasis on physical healing and far too little on the cross of the Lord Jesus Christ, repentance from sin amongst believers and genuine conversions amongst the unsaved. Too often it also seems that there is no interest or understanding of the signs of the times and the imminence of our Lord Jesus' return, even amongst the leadership. We need to be very careful in evaluating claims of extraordinary growth or revival and, amongst other enquiries, ask the vital question of whether it is producing real holiness of character amongst its adherents. If it is not, we can be quite sure that the movement is not of God.

Amongst those warning today's believers about the ecumenical and charismatic movements can be found sincere cessationists. Many of their writings can be found online. They make some excellent points about how the charismatic movement has been a powerful tool in forwarding the ecumenical agenda. For example, there are Catholic charismatics and charismatics in most of the apostate Protestant denominations. These are usually much more concerned about creating unity than faithful teaching, but it is not a unity based on God's Word and therefore is not of the Holy Spirit. Nevertheless, the unfortunate mistake cessationists make is to assume that the very foundation of the original charismatic movement was flawed. In their thinking, there is no such thing as a separate baptism with the Holy Spirit for believers and there are no supernatural gifts in operation today. Therefore, they reason, the movement was flawed from the beginning. In this way they fall into the trap that we looked at in chapter 6, namely that of correcting error with further error. The praiseworthy endeavour to warn the saints about spiritual deception is achieved at the cost of denying a very important truth. This can result in the uncharitable and indiscriminate labelling of those who believe in a separate baptism with the Holy Spirit alongside today's heretics and deceivers. Thus many godly and gifted men are grossly misrepresented when cessationists tar them with the same broad brush that they apply to the multitude of false teachers within the modern charismatic movement. What would they have made of C H Spurgeon's unostentatious use of a clearly supernatural gift (see chapter 4) that led to a man's conversion? Was Spurgeon a deceived charismatic? We think not!

In the face of misrepresentation by cessationists, we need only compare their assemblies with the Church as she should be, described in the book of Acts. Has the doctrine and practice of cessationists produced the vibrant spiritual life and resulting conversions we read of there? Clearly not. The truth is that conversions in such assemblies are all too rare.

There are still some Biblically faithful assemblies that, if pressed, would perhaps describe themselves as charismatic. They simply teach that the baptism with the Holy Spirit is distinct from conversion and that His gifts are available to the Church today.

It is obvious that the charismatic movement was targeted by Satan at an early stage in a way that staid, cessationist meetings were not. How do we account for this? It is surely that Satan has very little to fear from dead orthodoxy, but much of which to be afraid when a Church is truly empowered by the Holy Spirit and holding fast to the Word of God. The charismatic movement has been gradually infiltrated by sensual, experience-orientated professing Christians who have little time for sound doctrine. This does not excuse the leadership who should test all things according to God's Word, reject the false and hold fast to the true. Further to this, those inclined to introduce false doctrine and practice should be disciplined and, if necessary, excluded.

**Looking for Greener Grass**

There is a scenario that can easily arise within a cessationist assembly that is a potential danger to spiritually hungry young Christians. Many will have grown up within the assembly, but there can come a point when they realise that, if the Bible is true, there must be more to the Christian life than the rather predictable and unproductive status quo that surrounds them. Perhaps they have either heard or read about the baptism with the Holy Spirit and have a keen awareness that the whole matter is suppressed within their own assembly.

Upon reaching adulthood, some have launched out into the 'wilderness' to start their own fellowships, unrestricted by dogmatic cessationism. The danger comes when this venture is undertaken without the oversight of mature and godly leaders who are experienced in the Word, the things of the Holy Spirit and Satan's activity in that realm. The Devil has an array of subtle spiritual deceptions with which to ensnare the hungry but unwary seeker of greener grass.

This author was told of a situation very similar to the foregoing, where those involved were soon immersed in spiritual deception. They had embraced a phenomenon that emerged from the so-called Lakeland 'revival', in which professing Christians were reporting that their standard dental fillings had been miraculously turned to gold. Even if this was true, can any believer, with even a modicum of Biblical understanding, believe that God would be glorified by such a trifling sign or that this phenomenon would prompt sinners to repent and turn to Christ? It is this sort of thing that brings the truth of the baptism with the Holy Spirit into disrepute and causes many to reject it.

Such folly is not inevitable though. What is needed is mature and godly leadership by those who know the Word of God and test all things by it. When this happens, the blessing of God comes down upon the fellowship and spiritual barrenness is turned into fruitfulness for His glory.

## Purpose Driven Church, Emergent Church and The New Spirituality

These movements are having a tremendous impact on the modern church. Much has been written to warn about the dangers of them and some excellent documentaries clearly reveal their deceptive agenda.

In short, they are powerful vehicles for bringing a flood of un-Biblical teachings and practices into the professing church. It will be no surprise to the discerning believer that the teachings in these movements are completely compatible with New Age 'spirituality'. Their agenda fits hand-in-glove with the multi-faith, ecumenical strategy that is leading to the apostate one-world religion clearly prophesied for the end of this present Age.

We mention these to warn any reader who might be tempted to look in that direction for help in reversing the decline of their own church. The only safe place to look is into the Word of God, with a willingness to be corrected by it and then to wait upon God in prayer for an outpouring of His Holy Spirit. If your church is already involved with any of these movements or using their literature, it is almost certainly time to leave. I say 'almost' certainly, because it would be right to challenge the leadership with your concerns first. If they listened and repented by turning back to Biblical teaching, all would be well. Sadly, it has to be said that such an outcome is rare indeed.

It needs to be emphasised that, for all their talk about spirituality, the teaching and practice of these movements bears no relation to the Biblical teaching of baptism with the Holy Spirit. Indeed, their 'gospel' is not the Biblical Gospel of God's saving grace and therefore cannot save anyone. This is also true of the Roman Catholic Church, which preaches a different 'gospel'. They will sometimes use the phrase, 'baptised with the Holy Spirit', to describe their own 'charismatics', but mean something entirely different by it. Subtly changing the meanings of words and phrases characterises this age of shams in the religious as well as the political world. We need to remember that, according to the Bible, the only people who can be baptised with the Holy Spirit are those who have already been saved by believing the Biblical Gospel.

## SPIRITUAL GIFTS

I have deliberately omitted from this book any teaching on the gifts of the Holy Spirit. This is because, until one has received the baptism with the Holy Spirit, one cannot possess any of these gifts to require instruction in their use. It would be like instructing a soldier in the use of equipment that he had not yet collected from the armoury. The theory might be interesting, but it would be of no practical use to him at that point in time. The priority must be for believers to be told the truth about the baptism with the Holy Spirit and exhorted to seek God for it.

For those who have already been baptised with the Holy Spirit and for those whom I pray will be after being stirred to seek God for it, there is very good written and recorded teaching on the gifts available from reputable ministries.

## FINALLY, WHAT CAN YOU DO? WHAT WILL YOU DO?

The Trumpet of God will very soon be sounded, bringing the Church Age to a close. As He descends from Heaven, the Lord Jesus Christ will shout with a loud command at which all those who have died trusting in Him will be resurrected. After that, true Christians who are still alive at that point (which will probably include the great majority of us who are alive today) will be transformed, receiving our resurrection bodies without passing through death. We shall be caught up (raptured) into the clouds with those believers just raised from the dead, to meet the Lord Jesus Christ in the air. Having thus gathered His bride, the entirety of the true Church, He will take us to the home He has prepared for us in Heaven (1 Thessalonians 4:13-18, 1 Corinthians 15:51-55 and John 14:1-3).

This is a wonderful prospect for all of us who know and love the Lord Jesus Christ. Yet it would do us good to remember that, as believers, we shall then appear before the judgement seat of Christ (Romans 14:10, 2 Corinthians 5:10). This will not be a judgement of our sins because the Lord Jesus has already paid the price for those on Calvary's cross, hallelujah! Rather, it will be a judgement of our works and their true motivation, which will determine whether we are rewarded or not. Can we expect to be rewarded for seeking to maintain the status quo in our assembly, where that involves (whether admitted or not) the institutionalised quenching of the Holy Spirit? Can we expect to be rewarded if we are not prepared to take a stand on matters such as this, which might involve being ostracised? Are we prepared to stick our head above the parapet over *any* matters within the Church? We must all answer these questions honestly as before the Lord.

This book is a modest attempt to be a signpost pointing to the One who alone can baptise you with the Holy Spirit, namely the Lord Jesus Christ. How effective it will be, only He knows. It is my prayer that many readers will obtain the promise of the Father, the baptism with the Holy Spirit. Let us seek Him with the earnest desire that the Son of God may be glorified in and through us. If this is done by even a few, who knows whether God might grant a short season of revival in the Church, equipping her to reach the last of those to be saved before God's judgement falls on a sinful nation and world?

# WHAT IS THE GOSPEL AND SALVATION?

## The Ultimate Question

There is no more urgent question to settle than this for every man, woman and child on the planet. Concerns about such things as money, housing, food, clothing, education and jobs, although important, all pale into insignificance against the ultimate question of where we will spend eternity.

The tragedy is that, particularly in the West, so few people are even asking the question. Many today do not believe that they will have a conscious existence after death, whereas the Bible makes it abundantly clear that death is neither the cessation of existence nor consciousness. We have an eternal soul that will remain fully conscious after death and continue to exist in either Heaven or Hell. Not many generations ago, a much larger proportion of the population had at least *some* understanding of this sobering truth.

## God as Creator Denied

What has happened to render our generation so extraordinarily insensible to eternal matters? The answer lies in a wholesale shift of worldview that has increased its grip over each succeeding generation. Prior to that, the majority of people realised that there must be a Creator God, even if they did not profess to be Christian. What could account for such a dramatic change in worldview?

Ever since the theory of evolution was introduced by Darwin in 1859 as an alternative explanation for the origin of living organisms, including ourselves, it has gained increasing acceptance in the minds of modern men and women. It is now presented as science, which is very appealing to the many who desire to give their unbelief in God an 'intellectual' legitimacy. In recent decades many scientists have exposed the fatal flaws of evolutionary thinking and shown that it is not really science at all, but should more accurately be described as a philosophy or even a religion. Despite this, it is pushed relentlessly in our educational establishments and the media. Well-known names like Richard Dawkins and David Attenborough act as the 'high priests' of this anti-God religion. Dissenters are ridiculed mercilessly and enormous efforts are made to ensure that powerful evidence supporting the Biblical account of creation is suppressed in the public arena. It is a great mercy of God that various creation ministries have been set up to make widely available the scientific evidence for creation and to expose the fraudulent pseudo-science of evolution. However, the Bible makes it quite clear that even without the detailed evidence available from such ministries, the existence of the visible creation around us is quite sufficient to prove the existence of God.

*For the invisible things of him from the creation of the world are clearly seen, being understood by the things that are made, even his eternal power and Godhead; so that **they are without excuse:** (Romans 1:20)*

Without excuse! That is precisely how God views the multitudes of men and women in this generation who either deny His existence or make only a nominal acknowledgement of Him. The Word of God does not soft-pedal in its description of such people:

*__The fool__ hath said in his heart, There is no God. They are corrupt, they have done abominable works, there is none that doeth good. (Psalms 14:1)*

*Professing themselves to be wise, __they became fools__, (Romans 1:22)*

If ever there was a generation that professed to be wise, and yet in reality were fools, it is ours. The inevitable result of evolutionary brainwashing over the last one and a half centuries is a modern generation that has lost virtually all God-consciousness. A consequence of this is loss of any sense of accountability for our actions in this life. This inevitably leads to a climate of increasing lawlessness and moral decay from the lowest in society to those holding high office. Our nation has been plumbing the depths of sin for many years now. In 1967 the murder of unborn children was legalised with the Abortion Act. Since then the downhill slide has accelerated to the point where our Government now believes that it has the authority to redefine marriage in opposition to God's clear definition of that institution. There are even many claiming to be Christians who support such wilful rebellion against God, thus unwittingly fulfilling the very End Time Bible prophecies that they refuse to take seriously.

## The Bible is the Word of God

The Bible declares itself to be the Word of God.

*All scripture is given by inspiration of God, and is profitable for doctrine, for reproof, for correction, for instruction in righteousness:* (2 Timothy 3:16)

*For the prophecy came not in old time by the will of man: but holy men of God spake as they were moved by the Holy Ghost.* (2 Peter 1:21)

There is overwhelming evidence to support that the Bible is exactly what it claims to be. Unbeknown to most people, there are many artefacts in the British Museum that confirm the historical accuracy of much of the Old Testament. There is also very impressive manuscript evidence for the New Testament. In fact, from a variety of disciplines such as mathematics and science there is more than enough evidence to corroborate the veracity of the Bible for any *honest* enquirer. Perhaps the most impressive evidence, though, lies in the extraordinary accuracy with which many specific prophecies have been fulfilled. The first advent and subsequent ministry of the Lord Jesus Christ fulfilled with one hundred percent accuracy numerous Old Testament prophecies concerning Him. It has been demonstrated many times that the probability of one man fulfilling all of these prophecies by chance is effectively zero.

The unfulfilled prophecies of the Bible are mainly concerned with events that will bring this present age to a close. This will culminate in the Second Coming of the Lord

Jesus Christ to save Israel from destruction at the hands of the world's armies and to set up the kingdom of God on Earth. Again, these prophecies are very detailed. For the first time in mankind's history, *all* of the ingredients needed for the fulfilment of these prophecies are in place. Before 1948, there was no nation of Israel for the Lord Jesus Christ to return to. Today, in 2014, the Jewish nation exists, amidst much clamour and opposition. 'Natural' disasters and earthquakes are increasing exponentially in frequency, sexual immorality is rife, the homosexual agenda is forced on society, nations are losing their sovereignty to a world government plan and much of the professing church is falling away from the truth of the Bible into all manner of false teaching. All of these signs are very clear indicators that the end of this present age is upon us. Sadly, many choose to remain ignorant of these things. However, burying our heads in the sand will not absolve us from our responsibility to respond to and obey the Gospel.

Why have we been so emphatic about the Bible being the Word of God? Simply because God's message of salvation (i.e. the Gospel) and true Christianity are defined solely by the Word of God and not by any Church, tradition, theological college, clergyman or pastor. Much less is it defined by the Vatican, the Watchtower or any other cult headquarters. It is getting increasingly difficult in our day to find a church that faithfully preaches God's way of salvation. Many of today's churches should have a large spiritual health warning on their noticeboards. It is tragic to see multitudes deceived into thinking that they are in a right standing with God whilst they attend apostate churches or cults such as the Jehovah's Witnesses and willingly imbibe a message that cannot save anyone. In all likelihood, the majority will find out too late that they are still in their sins as God's judgement overtakes them. Many remain in such churches despite having been warned of the danger. The Bible gives the reason for this:

*(2 Timothy 4:1) I charge thee therefore before God, and the Lord Jesus Christ, who shall judge the quick and the dead at his appearing and his kingdom;*

*(2 Timothy 4:2)* **Preach the word**; *be instant in season, out of season; reprove, rebuke, exhort with all longsuffering and doctrine.*

*(2 Timothy 4:3)* **For the time will come when they will not endure sound doctrine**; *but after their own lusts shall they heap to themselves teachers, having itching ears;*

*(2 Timothy 4:4)* **And they shall turn away their ears from the truth, and shall be turned unto fables.**

This prophecy from the Bible is being fulfilled with alarming rapidity in our day. Even within some of the so-called 'evangelical' church, false teachers tickle the ears of professing Christians with what they want to hear rather than what they need to hear. Far too few churches teach faithfully the truth about creation and refute evolution, declare unequivocally that Jesus Christ is the *only* way of salvation and warn people of the significance of the signs all around us that point to the nearness of His return. The Bible is the sole authority for true Christian faith and we follow the crowd in doubting it or departing from it at our peril.

### The True History of Man

Man was created; he did not evolve. The widespread and aggressive denial of this truth is a foundational component of the wholesale falling away from the Faith that is so clearly prophesied in the Bible for the closing days of this Age. If you want to be saved from the coming judgement of God, you will need to stop listening to the 'wisdom' of men, whether secular or 'religious', and start listening to what God has said in His Word.

The Genesis account of creation and the early history of mankind are to be taken literally, whatever today's scoffers may be saying. The Lord Jesus Christ Himself affirmed this:

*And he answered and said unto them,* **Have ye not read,** *that* **he which made them at the beginning** *made them male and female,* *(Matthew 19:4)*

In these words to the unbelieving Pharisees, the Lord Jesus refers them to the book of Genesis, which He uses as being authoritative. In another exchange with the religious hierarchy, He said the following:

*(John 5:46) For had ye believed Moses, ye would have believed me: for he wrote of me.*
*(John 5:47) But* **if ye believe not his writings, how shall ye believe my words?**

The potency of Jesus' words here should not be overlooked. Moses wrote the book of Genesis as he was led by the Holy Spirit. The Lord Jesus is effectively telling His hearers that if they do not believe Moses' writings, they will not be able to believe His words. This throws an interesting light on many a modern church which claims to be following the Lord Jesus Christ, whilst denying His Word about origins in Genesis. We need to be careful which 'Jesus' we are following: the true, Biblical Jesus or a 'Jesus' that suits our own preferences.

*(2 Corinthians 11:3)  But I fear, lest by any means, **as the serpent beguiled Eve through his subtilty**, so your minds should be corrupted from the simplicity that is in Christ.*

*(2 Corinthians 11:4)  For if he that cometh preacheth **another Jesus**, whom we have not preached, or if ye receive **another spirit**, which ye have not received, or **another gospel**, which ye have not accepted, ye might well bear with him.*

Notice how the Apostle Paul treats Genesis as literal history in his reference to Eve being deceived by the serpent. He goes on to warn of the very real danger of following 'another Jesus' by sitting under the ministry of a false teacher. Is it really likely that those modern church leaders who deny the literal historicity of Genesis are wiser than the Lord Jesus Christ and the Apostle Paul?

Please read the early chapters of Genesis and receive them with strong faith. The good news of salvation through the Lord Jesus Christ makes no sense at all unless the early history of mankind as recorded in Genesis is literally true. Adam and Eve were created perfect and lived in a perfect environment, but they soon failed the only moral test God put before them. Their fall into sin was our fall. The Bible is emphatic that death was not a part of the original creation; it came in solely as a consequence of sin. We are all born into this world as sinners because of the fact of 'original sin'. We are incapable of fully obeying God's perfect Law, even if we wanted to. The evidence of this is plain to see as we watch the news night after night or observe how children turn out who have not been trained and disciplined to restrain the natural tendency to selfishness and wrongdoing that is in them. We have all broken and continue to break God's Law for which there is a very real and terrifying penalty to pay. Many today are hardly affected when they are told this because they have become anaesthetized to the fear of God. Their minds have been darkened and blinded from years of accepting an entirely false worldview; a worldview that seeks to explain away the creation around us without a Creator. As we saw earlier in this appendix, the Bible teaches that the visible creation makes it obvious that there must be a Creator God, leaving men and women without excuse.

## Spotlight on Man's Number One Problem

In our national life we expect our judges and magistrates to mete out appropriate punishments for lawbreakers. If they do not, there is a public outcry because justice has not been done. How strange it is then, that when it comes to breaking God's Law, we imagine that it should be entirely different. One popular notion is that as long as our 'good' deeds outweigh our bad deeds all will be well. By applying that thinking to the court room situation, someone guilty of armed robbery might escape jail by pointing to their many years of charitable work prior to the crime. We can all readily see the absurdity of that hypothetical scenario. There is a penalty for armed robbery and no amount of 'good' works prior to or after the offence makes any difference to the perpetrator's guilt.

The principle is the same, but to an infinitely higher degree, with God's laws that we have all broken. It is a solemn thing to break the law of the land, but who can begin to estimate the awful predicament of those who have broken the Law of the God who created the universe and everything in it? This God is holy, which means that He is set apart from and far above sinful mankind. He is perfect purity and righteousness, He is light and in Him is no darkness at all.

So just how many of us have broken God's Law? God gives us the answer in His Word:

*For **all have sinned**, and come short of the glory of God;* (Romans 3:23)

Many of us today deceive ourselves as to our true nature, by comparing ourselves with others. We reason that because we may not have murdered, raped, robbed a bank or committed adultery, we are basically 'good' people. Our fatal mistake is our definition of the word 'good'. We give it a meaning that enables us to feel at ease with ourselves. God has a very different definition of the word 'good'.

*(Matthew 19:16) And, behold, one came and said unto him,* **Good** *Master* (teacher), **what good thing shall I do**, *that I may have eternal life?*
*(Matthew 19:17) And he* (Jesus) *said unto him, Why callest thou me* **good? there is none good but one, that is, God***: but if thou wilt enter into life, keep the commandments.*

In this exchange between the Saviour and the 'Rich Young Ruler', Jesus corrects his understanding of the word 'good' and teaches that it can only be rightly applied to God. The following further quotes from the Scriptures clearly teach that true goodness is not to be found in anyone other than God.

*(Romans 3:10) As it is written,* **There is none righteous, no, <u>not one</u>***:*
*(Romans 3:11) There is none that understandeth, there is none that seeketh after God.*
*(Romans 3:12) They are all gone out of the way, they are together become unprofitable;* **there is none that doeth good, no, <u>not one</u>.**

To be acceptable to God we need to be good, which, in its true definition, means total perfection. We have just read that there is not a single person on this planet that meets that standard. This is the bad news and it could hardly be worse. Until we are ready to admit that we are helpless sinners deserving of God's punishment, we will remain in our sins with the certain prospect of God's judgement ahead of us. If we refuse to believe the bad news about our sin, we will reject the good news of God's message of salvation.

## God's Solution to our Problem

We have all sinned against an infinite and holy God by breaking His Law. The penalty for this is also infinite.

*For the wages of sin is death (Romans 6:23a)*

We have already seen that death is not the cessation of being. The penal death spoken of in this verse means a conscious existence banished from Heaven in a place of eternal torment and misery often translated in our Bible as Hell. Because God is a righteous Judge, He *must* judge sin in order to be consistent with His holy nature. Clearly, we are unable to pay the penalty for sin, so how can a righteous God save us from such an awful doom?

This is where the wonderful message of God's grace and mercy comes in. Before the foundation of the world, God had a plan to rescue men and women from their foreseen ruin in sin. As we have already seen, for a sinner to go free, the righteous penalty of the Law must be paid. If we cannot pay that price, where will the payment come from?

*Christ died for our sins in accordance with the Scriptures* (1 Corinthians 15:3b)

In these few short words we are told the astonishing truth that Jesus Christ has died for *our* sins. Putting it another way, Jesus Christ became our substitute, dying the death that should rightfully be ours when he died on the cross nearly 2000 years ago. This has always been God's plan to save men and women from judgement. Perhaps the best known of all Bible verses puts it like this:

*For God so loved the world, that he gave his only begotten Son, that whosoever believeth in him should not perish, but have everlasting life.* (John 3:16)

We should not just skim quickly through these words but read them *very carefully*, seeking to understand what God is saying to us through them. God's love for mankind is the reason that in an act of pure grace, He sent His Son down to earth to lay down His life for the sins of the whole world. As a result, those who believe on Jesus Christ will not perish but have everlasting life. To perish is not merely a reference to physical death, but to eternal conscious punishment in Hell. Before moving on further we must understand what is meant by the grace of God. Grace in that sense can best be described as undeserved favour. When we are saved by trusting or believing on the Lord Jesus Christ, we are saved by grace.

*(Ephesians 2:8)  For **by grace** are ye saved **through faith**; and that not of yourselves: it is the gift of God:*
*(Ephesians 2:9)  **Not of works**, lest any man should boast.*

That we can be saved by the grace of God is the most

wonderful news imaginable. Consider carefully for a few moments that Jesus Christ, the Son of the living God, has already paid the full penalty for your sin and mine when He died on the cross. There is nothing at all that can be added to the price He has paid, which is why the second verse above says *"Not of works"*. This means that it is absolutely impossible to earn your salvation with 'good' works. The very moment we simply turn in faith to Him for the forgiveness of our sins, we shall be saved.

*(Acts 16:30b)  Sirs, what must I do to be saved?*
*(Acts 16:31)  And they said,* **Believe on the Lord Jesus Christ, and thou shalt be saved,** *and thy house.*

So we see that salvation is a free gift from God that cannot be earned by working for it or obtained by trusting in church membership or religious rituals of any kind. God's wonderful way of salvation can seem too good to be true, yet it *is* true.

One would think that such an offer would be taken up immediately by people in their millions, yet the reality is that, in the West, very few people are being saved. Such is the darkness that has enveloped people's minds that they have become blind to the obvious. As we said at the beginning of this appendix, once people deny God as the Creator, further folly quickly ensues and their whole thought-life becomes vain and futile. This author was in that condition for the first thirty-two years of his life until God, in His mercy and grace, led him to the Lord Jesus Christ for the forgiveness of his sins.

*Because that, when they knew God, they glorified him not as God, neither were thankful;* **but became vain in their imaginations, and their foolish heart was darkened.**
*(Romans 1:21)*

Another reason people turn their backs on God's offer of a full and free salvation is pride. The pride of the human heart is one of the terrible results of original sin. We would much rather *do* something to earn our salvation, so that we had something to boast about, than be a debtor to God's grace and mercy alone. This can be a particular problem for religious people who would rather trust in performing their church's various activities and rituals than simply trust in Christ's finished sacrifice for their sins.

Religion cannot save anyone, yet large numbers of modern churchgoers are deceived by liberal clergy into thinking that they will somehow be 'alright' in the end. Sadly, nothing could be further from the truth.

Another stumbling block for many is the existence of all the different world religions. Surely they cannot all be wrong, can they? Jesus said the following:

*... I am **the** way, **the** truth, and **the** life: **no man** cometh unto the Father, **but by me**.  (John 14:6)*

This is totally exclusive. He did not say that He was *a* way, but *the* way. The modern notion that all religions are just different paths to God does not stand up to even a cursory scrutiny. They are mutually contradictory and not one of them is able to deal with man's number one problem, sin. Their founders are dead and buried, never to be heard from again, whereas the tomb in which Jesus was laid is empty. The resurrection of Jesus Christ from the dead is a well attested fact of history.

*Neither is there salvation in any other: for **there is none***

***other name*** *under heaven given among men, whereby we must be saved.* *(Acts 4:12)*

Time is fast running out for all of us. None of us know when our life will end, because God does not promise us tomorrow. Furthermore, the apocalyptic events that will end this present age will commence suddenly, like a thief in the night. All indicators point to the likelihood that this will be well before the end of the natural lifespan of most readers.

Having read this far, if you have never before turned to God for His mercy and forgiveness of your sins, beware of putting it off until that fatal 'tomorrow'. It is a sobering truth that multitudes have entered Hell after dying in their sins, assuming that they always had 'tomorrow' to get right with God.

*For he saith, I have heard thee in a time accepted, and in the day of salvation have I succoured thee:* ***behold, now is the accepted time; behold, now is the day of salvation.***
*(2 Corinthians 6:2)*

*For* ***whosoever shall call upon the name of the Lord <u>shall be saved</u>***. *(Romans 10:13)*